DAILY MATH PRACTICE

Grade 3

Daily Math Practice provides a structured approach to building and reviewing your students' mathematics skills.

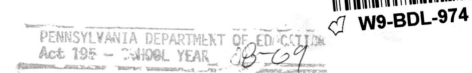

W9-BDL-974

PENNSYLVANIA DEPARTMENT OF EDUCATION
Act 195 – SCHOOL YEAR 08-69

Daily Skill
Practice one skill every day for a week

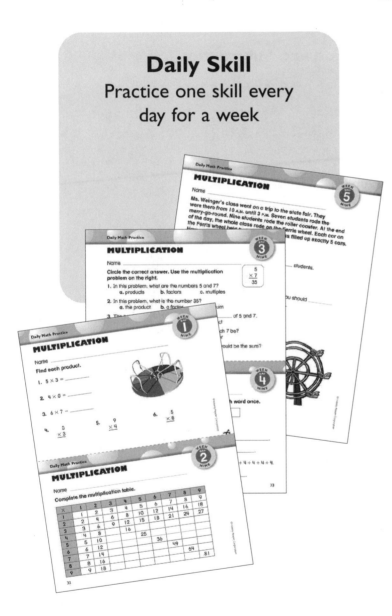

Monthly Review
Review skills learned each month

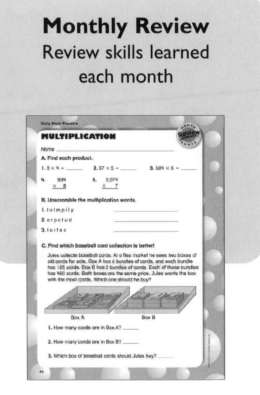

ISBN: 9–780837–483900
1 2 3 4 5 / 10 09 08

Table of Contents

Using This Book 4–5

Month 1: Place Value
Week 1 6
Week 2 9
Week 3 12
Week 4 15
Month 1 Review 18

Month 2: Addition and Subtraction
Week 5 19
Week 6 22
Week 7 25
Week 8 28
Month 2 Review 31

Month 3: Multiplication
Week 9 32
Week 10 35
Week 11 38
Week 12 41
Month 3 Review 44

Month 4: Division
Week 13 45
Week 14 48
Week 15 51
Week 16 54
Month 4 Review 57

Month 5: Geometry
Week 17 58
Week 18 61
Week 19 64
Week 20 67
Month 5 Review 70

Month 6: Measurement

Week 21 71
Week 22 74
Week 23 77
Week 24 80
Month 6 Review 83

Month 7: Fractions

Week 25 84
Week 26 87
Week 27 90
Week 28 93
Month 7 Review 96

Month 8: Graphs, Data, and Probability

Week 29 97
Week 30 100
Week 31 103
Week 32 106
Month 8 Review 109

Month 9: Patterns

Week 33 110
Week 34 113
Week 35 116
Week 36 119
Month 9 Review 122

Answer Key 123

Using This Book

In this reproducible book you'll find daily math practice with essential third grade skills. It's a valuable classroom resource packed with quick and easy-to-use activities designed to practice skills, use math vocabulary, and apply skills. You can use these activities in a variety of classroom situations—as daily warm-ups, quick assessment tools, or helpful reviews.

This book's organization features 9 months of practice activities. Each month includes four weeks of daily activities. Each week includes activities that: Practice the Skill, Use the Words, and Apply the Skill. Each month ends with a review of the skills featured in the month.

Each week includes five days of activities.

Days 1 and 2 provide students with the opportunity to **Practice the Skill**.

Days 3 and 4 focus on math vocabulary and involve activities that offer students the opportunity to **Use the Words**.

Day 5 provides students with the opportunity to **Apply the Skill** they have practiced in a problem-solving setting.

At the end of each four-week set there is a **Monthly Review**. Each monthly review includes activities that review the skills and vocabulary taught during the month.

Daily Practice

When planning your daily routine, try one or more of these management techniques.

- Make copies of the daily activity page for students to complete each morning. Review the completed page as a whole group.

- Distribute copies of each daily page to individual students or to small groups. You might choose to have students work together for Day 1 and Day 3 and then independently for Day 2, Day 4, and Day 5. When students work independently, encourage them to exchange work with a partner and compare and discuss their answers. Or, review the correct responses together as a large group.

- Create transparencies and use an overhead projector to complete the work in a large group. Ask volunteers to help complete each item. Try completing Day 1 as a whole-class activity to introduce the week's skill. Then have students work independently or in pairs to complete Day 2. Use Day 3 as a whole-class activity to introduce the week's new words. Then have students work independently or in pairs to complete Day 4. Finally have students complete Day 5 independently or with a partner. Talk about the correct responses together as a large group.

- Direct students to complete some activities for homework. Encourage students to share their work at home.

Extension Activities

Helping your students develop and build mathematical skills and thinking is an ongoing process. This practice book is a terrific tool to help you reach your educational goals. Here are some other things you can do every day to help students develop number sense and mathematical thinking.

Writing in Mathematics

Writing helps students learn and remember. Have each student create a Math Journal. Create opportunities for students to write for different purposes.

• Recording what they have learned

• Explaining their thinking

• Creating new problems

• Listing questions they may still have about a concept or skill

Learning Vocabulary

Go over new words with the students. Help them pronounce the words correctly and explain that they will use these words in the Day 3 and Day 4 activities. If students are keeping a Math Journal, have them write the words and their definitions in their Journal as the words are found in the activities.

Talking About It

Have students talk aloud about what they have learned. This helps them build confidence in mathematics and helps educators better assess students' understanding of skills and concepts. It also helps family members understand what skills the children are learning.

Inch/Centimeter Rulers

Make copies of the inch and centimeter rulers for students to cut out and use for the activities that require students to measure the length of objects.

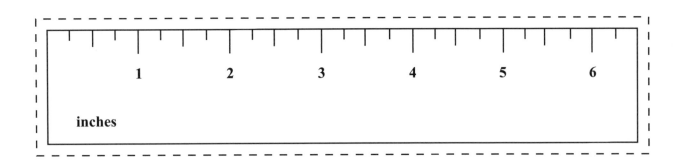

inches

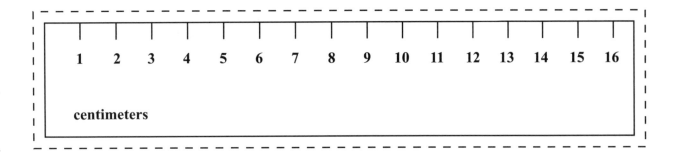

centimeters

PLACE VALUE

Name _____

Write the number that comes next.

1. 143 144 145 146 _____

2. 2,003 2,004 2,005 2,006 _____

3. 3,165 3,166 3,167 3,168 _____

4. 8,307 8,308 8,309 8,310 _____

5. 4,638 4,639 4,640 4,641 _____

PLACE VALUE

Name _____

Write each number in standard form.

1. five thousand, three hundred fifty-seven _____

2. nine thousand, nine hundred seventy-nine _____

3. one thousand, one hundred thirty-one _____

4. one thousand, six hundred forty _____

5. six thousand, four _____

PLACE VALUE

Name _____

Write each number in word form.

1. 9,529   _____

2. 7,503   _____

3. 6,010   _____

4. 1,517   _____

5. 3,142   _____

PLACE VALUE

Name _____

Fill in the blanks with words from the box. Use each word once.

word form	standard form	thousands	hundreds	place value

1. The number 5,432 has 4 _____.

2. Seven hundred eleven is written in _____.

3. The value of a digit depends on its _____.

4. The number 8,090 has 8 _____.

5. The number 1,599 is written in _____.

PLACE VALUE

Name _____

Which city has the tallest building? For a long time, the Empire State Building in New York was the tallest. It is one thousand, two hundred fifty feet tall. Today, many buildings are taller. The Jin Mao Building in Shanghai is 1,381 feet tall. The Sears Tower in Chicago is 1,451 feet tall. Kuala Lumpur has two towers that are each 1,483 feet tall. Even taller is a building called the Taipei 101 Tower. It is in Taipei, Taiwan, and it is 1,667 feet tall!

1. Write the height of the Empire State Building in standard form.

_____

2. Write the height of the Sears Tower in word form.

_____

3. Write the height of the Jin Mao Building in word form.

_____

4. Write the height of the Taipei 101 Tower in word form.

_____

5. The digit 1 shows up two times in the height of the Sears Tower. Do they have different values? Explain your answer.

_____

PLACE VALUE

Name _____

What is the place value of the digit 8 in each number?

1. 8,234   _____

2. 1,008   _____

3. 482   _____

4. 3,860   _____

5. 87   _____

PLACE VALUE

Name _____

Write the value of the underlined digit.

1. 6,892   _____

2. 3,049   _____

3. 1,774   _____

4. 9,266   _____

5. 2,548   _____

PLACE VALUE

WEEK
DAY
3
TWO

Name _____

Fill in the blanks with words from the box. You can use the words more than once.

thousands	hundreds	tens	ones

1. In 283, the digit 2 is in the _____ place.

2. In 3,406, the digit 6 is in the _____ place.

3. In 1,045, the digit 1 is in the _____ place.

4. In 7,010, the digit 1 is in the _____ place.

5. In 251, the digit 1 is in the _____ place.

PLACE VALUE

WEEK
DAY
4
TWO

Name _____

Fill in the blanks.

1. In 8,176, the digit _____ is in the hundreds place.

2. In 1,933, the digit _____ is in the ones place.

3. The digit in the thousands place in 3,076 is _____.

4. In 4,452, the digit _____ is in the tens place.

5. The digit in the hundreds place in 3,076 is _____.

PLACE VALUE

Name _____

How Big Are the Planets?

Planet	Mercury	Venus	Earth	Mars
Width (in Miles)	3,032	7,519	7,926	4,194

1. Which planet's width has the greatest digit in the hundreds place?

   _____

2. Which planet's width has a 3 in the thousands place?

   _____

3. What is the value of the digit 9 in the width of Venus?

   _____

4. What is the value of the digit 9 in the width of Earth?

   _____

5. The digit 4 shows up two times in the width of Mars. Write the value for each digit.

   _____   _____

11

PLACE VALUE

Name _____

Compare the numbers. Write < or > in each .

1. 9,346 ◯ 146

2. 207 ◯ 2,007

3. 500 ◯ 499

4. 5,899 ◯ 6,012

5. 233 ◯ 2,033

PLACE VALUE

Name _____

Write the numbers in order from least to greatest.

1.	9,241	3,001	2,899	576
	_____	_____	_____	_____
2.	4,772	903	4,769	8,005
	_____	_____	_____	_____
3.	1,355	78	952	8,067
	_____	_____	_____	_____
4.	9,999	2,363	9	99
	_____	_____	_____	_____

PLACE VALUE

Name _____

Fill in the blanks with words from the box.
You can use the words more than once.

equal to	greater than	less than

1. 7,799 is _____ 7,801.

2. 6,012 is _____ 3,158.

3. Six thousand, five hundred eighty-six is _____ 6,586.

4. 3,782 is _____ 3,792.

5. 2,327 is _____ three thousand, three hundred seventy-two.

PLACE VALUE

Name _____

Compare the numbers. Write <, >, or = in each ◯ .

1. 5,001 ◯ 501   **2.** 3,982 ◯ 3,982

3. 1,644 ◯ 1,634   **4.** 7,529 ◯ 7,529

5. 199 ◯ 299

PLACE VALUE

Name _____

John and Rafael are friends. They live in different towns and go to different schools. They drew pictures of their schools. Then they wrote the number of students who go to their school.

John's school
1,728

Rafael's school
1,736

Which school has the greater number of students?

1. Compare the digits in the thousands place. Can you tell which school has the greater number of students? Why or why not?

   _____

   _____

2. Compare the digits in the hundreds place. Can you tell which school has the greater number of students? Why or why not?

   _____

   _____

3. Compare the digits in the tens place. Can you tell which school has the greater number of students? Why or why not?

   _____

   _____

4. Do you need to compare the digits in the ones place? Why or why not?

   _____

   _____

5. Compare the number of students in the two schools.
   Use the symbols < or >.

   _____

PLACE VALUE

Name _____

**Look at each number in expanded form.
Circle its value in standard form.**

1. 6,000 + 500 + 20 + 7   6,537   6,725   6,527

2. 1,000 + 900 + 2   1,920   1,902   192

3. 3,000 + 700 + 70 + 6   3,767   3,607   3,776

4. 9,000 + 200 + 10 + 8   9,218   9,280   920

5. 5,000 + 1   51   5,000   5,001

PLACE VALUE

Name _____

Write each number in expanded form.

1. 7,199 = _____ + _____ + _____ + _____

2. 9,313 = _____ + _____ + _____ + _____

3. 1,127 = _____ + _____ + _____ + _____

4. 4,952 = _____ + _____ + _____ + _____

5. 6,284 = _____ + _____ + _____ + _____

PLACE VALUE

Name _____

Fill in the blanks with words from the box. Use each word once. Then, complete the problem.

word	standard	expanded

1. The number 7,547 is in _____ form.

In expanded form it would be _____ + _____ + _____ + _____.

2. Two thousand, twenty-six is in _____ form.

In standard form it would be _____.

3. 3,000 + 700 + 60 + 1 is in _____ form.

In standard form it would be _____.

PLACE VALUE

Name _____

Fill in the blanks with words from the box. You can use a word more than once.

ones	tens	hundreds	thousands

1. The digit 1 in 6,193 is in the _____ place.

2. The digit 4 in 5,449 is in the _____ place and the _____ place.

3. The digit 3 in 3,082 is in the _____ place.

4. The digit 0 in 9,101 is in the _____ place.

5. The digit 9 in 4,089 is in the _____ place.

PLACE VALUE

Name _____

Mark the objects to show the number.

1. Perry runs a sports center called the Ping-Pong Palace. Last year, he used seven thousand, four hundred fifty-six Ping-Pong balls. Mark the Ping-Pong balls that show this number.

   5   700   60   4,000   400   6   50   7,000

2. Maya is having a giant party. All of her friends will be there. She will have one thousand, two hundred fifty-three balloons. Mark the balloons that show this number.

   8,000   200   5   50   1,000   30   3   500

3. The Capital City Jackals are a baseball team. Their manager needs to buy baseballs for the team for the season. He orders two thousand, eight hundred nine baseballs. Mark the baseballs that show this number.

   80   9   90   200   8,000   800   8   2,000

4. A stadium uses light bulbs for its giant scoreboard. The lights show the scores for all the other games. The scoreboard uses three thousand, one hundred eighty light bulbs. Mark the light bulbs that show this number.

   1,000   10   800   1   3,000   100   80   8

17

PLACE VALUE

Name _____

A. Compare the numbers using <, >, or =.

1. 9,076 ◯ 9,706   **2.** 2,399 ◯ 2,398   **3.** 6,274 ◯ 6,274

B. Compare the numbers. Fill in the blanks with words from the box. You can use a word more than once.

greater	less	ones	hundreds	thousands

1. You can tell that 7,821 is _____ than 7,933 by looking
at the _____ place.

2. You can tell that 4,511 is _____ than 8,632 by looking
at the _____ place.

3. You can tell that 8,474 is _____ than 8,473 by looking
at the _____ place.

C. The six longest rivers in the world are shown in the box. Put them in order, beginning with the longest. The first has been done for you.

Amazon 3,912 mi	Mississippi-Missouri 3,710 mi	Ob 3,459 mi
Yangtze 3,602 mi	Nile 4,180 mi	Yellow 2,900 mi

_____ Nile 4,180 mi

_____ _____

_____ _____

_____ _____

_____ _____

ADDITION AND SUBTRACTION

WEEK DAY **1** FIVE

Name _____

Find each sum.

1.   468
   + 511

2.   264
   + 1,523

3.   6,822
   + 2,176

4. $5,732 + $4,145 = _____

5. 3,618 + 5,271 = _____

ADDITION AND SUBTRACTION

WEEK DAY **2** FIVE

Name _____

Solve each problem by adding.

1. There are 1,261 boys and 1,307 girls at Smithfield School. There are

   _____ students at Smithfield School altogether.

2. An ocean liner sailed 2,573 miles in January. Then it sailed 3,116 miles

   in February. It sailed _____ miles in January and
   February combined.

3. A beekeeper has hives at two farms. At the first farm she counted
   3,744 bees. At the second farm she counted 6,135 bees. How many

   bees does the beekeeper have in total? _____.

ADDITION AND SUBTRACTION

Name _____

Read the problem. Then, fill in the blanks with words from the box. You may use a word more than once.

addends	sum	addition

There were 6,712 fans at the concert on Saturday and 3,284 fans on Sunday. How many fans went to the concerts over the weekend in all?

1. The words *in all* tell you that this problem can be solved using

_____.

2. To solve the problem, you must find the _____ of 6,712 and 3,284.

3. The numbers 6,712 and 3,284 are _____ you will have to add.

4. The _____ of 6,712 + 3,284 is 9,996.

© Weekly Reader Corporation

ADDITION AND SUBTRACTION

Name _____

Read each question. Circle the word or words that tell you that you will need to add. Then, write the answer.

1. What is the sum of $5,238 and $2,441? _____

2. How much is 3,242 plus 2,512? _____

3. Robert owns 1,673 baseball cards. Luis owns 1,225 cards. How many baseball cards do they own altogether? _____

4. The chickens in the first henhouse laid 2,736 eggs. The chickens in the second henhouse laid 2,162 eggs. What was the total number of eggs for both henhouses? _____

© Weekly Reader Corporation

ADDITION AND SUBTRACTION

Name _____

Two classes at Middlebury School collected pennies. The school was going to give the money from the collection to charity. At the end of two months, the students in one class collected 4,322 pennies. The students in the second class collected 3,626 pennies. How many pennies were collected in all?

1. Which operation do you need to use to find out how many pennies were collected in all? Circle the correct answer.

   a. subtraction   **b.** addition   **c.** multiplication

2. To find the sum of the two penny collections, which two numbers must you add?

   _____ and _____

3. Write a number sentence to show how you can find the sum.

   _____

4. In this problem, what are the numbers 4,322 and 3,626 called?

   _____

5. Write an addition problem to find the total number of pennies collected. Then, solve.

   _____

6. In a different month, each class collected the same number of pennies. If each class collected 1,341 pennies, how could you find the total number of pennies the classes collected that month? Write the problem and solve it.

   _____

ADDITION AND SUBTRACTION

WEEK
DAY
1
SIX

Name _____

Find each difference.

1.   593
   − 272

2. $5,834
   −   310

3.   9,765
   − 6,143

4. 1,918 − 803 = _____

5. $7,129 − $3,016 = _____

ADDITION AND SUBTRACTION

WEEK
DAY
2
SIX

Name _____

Use subtraction to solve each problem.

1. The Carson family plan to travel 3,793 miles. After one week they have gone 1,681 miles. How many more miles do they need to travel? _____

2. Ben has saved $2,416. He spends $205. How much money does he have left? _____

3. Farmer Green owns 2,472 chickens. He sells 1,350. How many chickens does he have left? _____

4. The Rand School bought 5,655 pencils. After two months it had given out 2,143. How many pencils does the school have left? _____

ADDITION AND SUBTRACTION

Name _____

Read the problems. Then, answer each question.

Jose has $4,388 in his savings account. He takes out $1,345. How much money is left in his account?

1. What words tell you that this is a subtraction problem?

_____

2. How much money is left in his account? _____

Sally has 6,752 pennies. Mary has 4,531 pennies. How many more pennies does Sally have?

3. What words tell you that this is a subtraction problem?

_____

4. How many more pennies does Sally have than Mary? _____

ADDITION AND SUBTRACTION

Name _____

Read the problems. Then, answer each question.

A bicycle team must ride 2,755 miles this year. So far, they have ridden 1,642 miles. How many more miles do they have to ride?

1. The words *how many more* tell you that you have to _____.

2. The bicycle team must ride _____ more miles.

Littleton has 8,675 people. Logan has 5,560 people. Find the difference between the number of people in the two towns.

3. The word _____ tells you this problem can be solved with subtraction.

4. To find the difference you must subtract _____ from _____.

ADDITION AND SUBTRACTION

Name _____

Jackson lives in Los Angeles, California. It is one of the country's biggest cities. He will take a trip to see his grandparents in Chicago, Illinois. He will also take a trip to Detroit to visit his uncle and aunt. The sign shows the distances. What is the difference between the two distances?

Los Angeles to Chicago about 2,018 miles ↗

Los Angeles to Detroit about 2,284 miles ↗

1. Which words tell you that this is a subtraction problem? Circle the correct answer.

   a. He will take a trip

   b. What is the difference

   c. It is about 2,284 miles

2. Which city is farther from Los Angeles: Detroit or Chicago? _____

3. Detroit is _____ miles from Los Angeles.

4. Chicago is _____ miles from Los Angeles.

5. To find the difference between the two distances you must subtract _____ from _____ .

6. Set up a problem to find out the difference between the two distances. Then, solve it.

7. The difference between the two distances is _____ .

ADDITION AND SUBTRACTION

Name _____

Find each sum. Regroup when needed.

1. 4,538
  + 2,324

2. $7,427
  + 1,931

3. 3,372
  + 5,838

4. 1,497 + 6,720 = _____

5. $8,051 + $1,769 = _____

ADDITION AND SUBTRACTION

Name _____

Find each sum. Regroup when needed.

1. How much is 3,907 plus 2,486? _____

2. What is the sum of 5,144 and 2,567? _____

3. If you add $7,184 to $1,931,
what is the total amount of money? _____

4. Calculate the sum of 4,766 and 3,257. _____

5. Find the sum of $6,380 and $1,905. _____

ADDITION AND SUBTRACTION

Name _____

Fill in the blanks with words from the box. Use each word once.

sum   altogether   add   addends   regroup

Juan has 1,646 stamps in his collection. He gets 565 more.
How many stamps does Juan have altogether?

1. The word _____ tells you that this is an addition problem.

2. To solve this problem you must _____ 1,646 and 565.

3. The answer to this problem is called the _____.

4. In this problem, the numbers 1,646 and 565 are called _____.

5. When you add the numbers in the ones place,
6 and 5, you get 11. That means you must _____.

© Weekly Reader Corporation

ADDITION AND SUBTRACTION

Name _____

Circle the word or words in each problem that tells you that you need to add. Then, find each sum.

1. Reggie ran the football for 1,862 yards. Paul ran the ball
1,451 yards. How many yards did they gain altogether? _____

2. The runners in the marathon drank 4,783 cups of water.
Last year they drank 4,532 cups. How many cups did
they drink in both years? _____

3. The Main Street movie theater sold 3,955 tickets last month.
The Elm Street movie theater sold 4,306 tickets in the
same month. What was the total number of tickets sold? _____

4. Steve has $2,034 in one bank account. He has $1,597
in another. What is the sum of both accounts? _____

© Weekly Reader Corporation

ADDITION AND SUBTRACTION

Name _____

One day each fall, a local bird-watching group does a hawk survey. They count the number of hawks they see on that day. Last year, the group counted a total of 3,902 hawks. This year, the number of hawks counted by the group was 2,879. How many hawks were counted in both years?

1. Set up a problem to show how you can add the numbers 3,902 and 2,879.

2. What happens when you add the digits in the ones place? Explain what you need to do.

_____

_____

3. What happens when you add the digits in the tens place? Explain what you need to do.

_____

_____

4. What happens when you add the digits in the hundreds place? Explain what you need to do.

_____

_____

5. What happens when you add the digits in the thousands place? Explain what you need to do.

_____

_____

6. How many hawks were counted in both years? _____

ADDITION AND SUBTRACTION

Name _____

Find each difference. Regroup when needed.

1. 4,247
  − 2,615

2. $7,219
  − 2,176

3. 1,232
  − 1,150

4. 9,627 − 7,940 = _____

5. $3,707 − $1,584 = _____

ADDITION AND SUBTRACTION

Name _____

Find each difference. Regroup when needed.

1. What is the difference between 5,108 and 2,371? _____

2. What is 6,127 take away 4,236? _____

3. How much is $7,804 minus $2,921? _____

4. How much greater is $2,374 than $1,962? _____

5. What is the difference between 3,428 and 2,399? _____

ADDITION AND SUBTRACTION

Name _____

Complete each subtraction problem using a word or words from the box. Use each word once.

difference	more	are left

1. There are 5,149 pairs of sneakers in a store. The store sells 1,305 pairs of the sneakers. How many pairs of sneakers _____?

2. The bus must travel 2,347 miles to reach its destination. It has already

gone 1,268 miles. How many _____ miles must it travel?

3. One river is 2,045 miles long. Another is 1,738 miles long. What is

the _____ between the lengths of the two rivers?

ADDITION AND SUBTRACTION

Name _____

Unscramble each set of letters to spell subtraction words.

1. a k e w a a t y   _____

2. s u m n i   _____

3. t r u b s a c t   _____

4. i d e r e n f c e f   _____

5. w h o a m n y   o r e m   _____

29

ADDITION AND SUBTRACTION

Name _____

The Statue of Liberty was a gift to the United States from France. It was presented in 1886 on Liberty Island, New York. At first, the statue served as a lighthouse. In 1902, the statue stopped being used as a lighthouse. How many years was the Statue of Liberty a lighthouse?

1. What operation should you use to solve this problem? _____

2. Write a problem to show how you would find the answer.

3. What happens when you try to subtract the 6 from the 2 in the ones place? What happens to the tens place? Explain your answer.

_____

_____

4. How would you describe regrouping to a friend?

_____

_____

5. What is the answer to the problem? Show your work.

_____

ADDITION AND SUBTRACTION

MONTH
Review
TWO

Name _____

A. Find each sum or difference. Regroup when needed.

1. $2,443
    + 3,506

2. 6,701
    + 1,198

3. $7,299
    − 1,421

4. 5,081 + 4,394 = _____

5. $6,869 − $5,341 = _____

B. Read the story. Then, solve the problems.

Two hot air balloons raced across the Atlantic Ocean. They took off from Washington, D.C., and headed toward London, England. After three days, Balloon A had gone 1,331 miles. Balloon B had gone 1,574 miles. The distance from Washington, D.C., to London is 3,669 miles.

1. To find the number of miles that Balloon A has left to travel,

    you must subtract _____ from _____. The difference

    is _____.

2. To find the number of miles that Balloon B has left to travel,

    you must subtract _____ from _____. The difference

    is _____.

C. Solve each addition or subtraction problem. Then, write the answer in the correct squares in the puzzle.

Across

2. 3,264
    + 2,871

4. 9,273
    − 8,261

6. 5,416
    + 2,383

Down

1. 8,478
    − 4,347

3. 6,839
    − 1,322

5. 1,163
    + 1,625

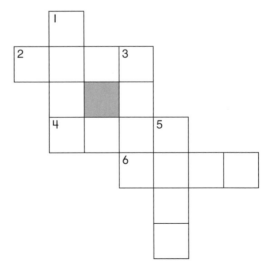

MULTIPLICATION

Name _____

Find each product.

1. 5 × 3 = _____

2. 4 × 0 = _____

3. 6 × 7 = _____

4.	3	5.	9	6.	5
	× 3		× 4		× 8

MULTIPLICATION

Name _____

Complete the multiplication table.

×	1	2	3	4	5	6	7	8	9
1	1	2	3	4	5	6	7	8	9
2	2	4	6	8	10	12	14	16	18
3	3	6	9	12	15	18	21	24	27
4	4	8		16					
5	5	10			25				
6	6	12				36			
7	7	14					49		
8	8	16						64	
9	9	18							81

MULTIPLICATION

Name _____

Circle the correct answer. Use the multiplication problem on the right.

$$\begin{array}{r} 5 \\ \times\, 7 \\ \hline 35 \end{array}$$

1. In this problem, what are the numbers 5 and 7?
   a. products   **b.** factors   **c.** multiples

2. In this problem, what is the number 35?
   a. the product   **b.** a factor   **c.** the sum

3. The product of 7 and 5 is the same as the _____ of 5 and 7.
   a. addend   **b.** factor   **c.** product

4. If you added $7 + 7 + 7 + 7 + 7$, what would each 7 be?
   a. an addend   **b.** a sum   **c.** a factor

5. If you added $5 + 5 + 5 + 5 + 5 + 5 + 5$, what would be the sum?
   a. 7   **b.** 35   **c.** 5×7

MULTIPLICATION

Name _____

Fill in the blanks with words from the box. Use each word once.

multiplication	factors	product	sum

$$4 \times 6 = \underline{\hspace{2cm}}$$

1. You can solve this problem using _____.

2. In this problem, the numbers 4 and 6 are _____.

3. The product of 4×6 is equal to the _____ of $4 + 4 + 4 + 4 + 4 + 4$.

4. In this problem, the number 24 is the _____.

MULTIPLICATION

Name _____

Ms. Weinger's class went on a trip to the state fair. They were there from 10 A.M. until 3 P.M. Seven students rode the merry-go-round. Nine students rode the roller coaster. At the end of the day, the whole class rode on the Ferris wheel. Each car on the Ferris wheel held 4 students. The class filled up exactly 5 cars. How many students are in the class?

Fill in the blanks.

1. Each car on the Ferris wheel holds _____ students.

2. The class filled exactly _____ cars.

3. To find the number of students in the class, you should _____ the number of students by the number of cars.

4. In this problem, the numbers _____ and _____ are the factors.

5. In this problem, the product is _____.

6. How many students are there in the class? _____

MULTIPLICATION

Name _____

Find each product.

1. $34 \times 3 =$ _____

2. $71 \times 9 =$ _____

3. $95 \times 1 =$ _____

4. $\begin{array}{r} 27 \\ \times\ 6 \\ \hline \end{array}$ 5. $\begin{array}{r} 54 \\ \times\ 8 \\ \hline \end{array}$

MULTIPLICATION

Name _____

Solve each problem by multiplying.

1. There are 8 football teams in the league. Each team has 21 players. How many football players are there in the league? _____

2. At Nancy's party she gave 2 balloons to each of her guests. There were 23 guests at the party. How many balloons did Nancy give out? _____

3. There are 4 children in the McCarthy family. Each child got a box of 64 crayons. How many crayons did they get altogether? _____

MULTIPLICATION

Name _____

Circle the best multiplication problem to use to estimate each problem.

1. 37 × 6	**a.** 40 × 6	**b.** 50 × 6	**c.** 35 × 10
2. 22 × 4	**a.** 30 × 5	**b.** 25 × 5	**c.** 20 × 4
3. 69 × 5	**a.** 70 × 5	**b.** 60 × 5	**c.** 96 × 5
4. 11 × 9	**a.** 12 × 10	**b.** 8 × 8	**c.** 10 × 10

- -

MULTIPLICATION

Name _____

Circle the correct answer.

If 86 students each read 5 books, how many books did they read altogether?

1. Which operation could you use to solve this problem?
    a. division   **b.** subtraction   **c.** multiplication

2. If you multiply 86 by 5, what is the product?
    a. 420   **b.** 340   **c.** 430

3. If you multiply 5 by 86, what is the product?
    a. 420   **b.** 430   **c.** 340

4. How many books did they read altogether?
    a. 430 books   **b.** 340 books   **c.** 420 books

MULTIPLICATION

Name _____

There are 52 weeks in a year. Charlie works on Saturdays mowing lawns. He makes $15 for every lawn he mows. During the winter, he makes money by shoveling snow. If Charlie saves 5 dollars every week, how much will he have saved after one year?

1. How much does Charlie save each week? _____

2. How many weeks are in a year? _____

3. What do you need to do to find out how much Charlie saved after one year? Circle the correct answer.

    a. Multiply the number of weeks by $15.

    b. Multiply the number of weeks by $5.

    c. Multiply $15 by $5.

4. Write a multiplication problem to show how much Charlie saved after one year.

5. How much will Charlie have saved after one year? _____

6. Charlie decides to save 6 dollars a week. What multiplication problem can he use to find out how much money he will save in a year? Write and solve a multiplication problem.

MULTIPLICATION

Name _____

Find each product.

1. $821 \times 3 =$ _____

2. $904 \times 0 =$ _____

3. $715 \times 2 =$ _____

4. $\quad 541$
   $\underline{\times \quad 7}$

5. $\quad 383$
   $\underline{\times \quad 6}$

MULTIPLICATION

Name _____

Solve by multiplying.

1. On Tuesday, 858 people bought tickets to the concert. Each person bought 2 tickets. How many tickets were sold that day? _____

2. A rancher has 207 horses. Each horse eats 7 buckets of grain a week. How many buckets of grain does the rancher need every week? _____

3. A department store is giving away free soap samples. They want to give out 950 samples a day. How many samples will they need for 5 days? _____

4. The Springfield School gives each of its students 4 notebooks at the start of the school year. There are 574 students in the school. How many notebooks are given out? _____

MULTIPLICATION

Name _____

Circle the correct answer.

A jet plane travels 435 miles an hour.
How many miles can it travel in 6 hours?

1. Which operation could you use to solve this problem?
    a. subtraction   **b.** division   **c.** multiplication

2. Which are the factors in this problem?
    a. 4 and 35   **b.** 6 and 435   **c.** 435

3. Which is greater: the product of 6×435 or the product of 435×6?
    a. They are the same.   **b.** 6×435 is greater   **c.** 435×6 is greater

4. What is the product of 6×435? How many miles can it travel in 6 hours?
    a. 2,610 mi   **b.** 2,106 mi   **c.** 2,600 mi

Daily Math Practice

MULTIPLICATION

Name _____

Circle the correct answer.

1. $8 \times 672 = 5,376$
    In this problem, 8 and 672 are the _____.
    a. products   **b.** factors   **c.** addends

2. $9 \times 109 = 981$
    The product is _____.
    a. 9   **b.** 109   **c.** 981

3. $6 \times 723 = 4,338$ $723 \times 6 = 4,338$
    In these two problems
    a. the factors are the same.
    b. the products are the same.
    c. both a and b.

MULTIPLICATION

Name _____

Jennifer needs 2,000 color copies of a picture by 4 P.M. The copy machine makes about 570 color copies in an hour. She starts copying at noon. That gives her 4 hours to make the copies. Will she be able to make them in time?

1. Jennifer wants to make _____ copies.

2. She has _____ hours to make her copies.

3. The machine makes _____ copies an hour.

4. You can solve this problem using the operation _____.

5. In this problem, _____ and _____ are the factors.

6. The product of _____ and _____ is _____.

7. Jennifer can make _____ copies in 4 hours.

8. Does Jennifer have enough time to maker her copies? _____

MULTIPLICATION

Name _____

Multiply.

1. $1{,}704 \times 6 =$ _____

2. $8{,}655 \times 2 =$ _____

3. $7{,}561 \times 8 =$ _____

4.
$$\begin{array}{r} 9{,}127 \\ \times 4 \\ \hline \end{array}$$

5.
$$\begin{array}{r} 1{,}403 \\ \times 9 \\ \hline \end{array}$$

MULTIPLICATION

Name _____

Solve by multiplying.

1. The round-trip distance from New York City to Miami is 2,194 miles. If a plane makes the round trip every day for 7 days, how many miles does it fly? _____

2. An auto factory made 8,361 cars. It takes 6 hours to make each car. How many hours did it take to make all the cars? _____

3. Jon saved $3,040 in one year. If he saves the same amount every year, how much will he have after 4 years? _____

4. A music website sold 8,549 downloads of a song. They charged $2 for each download. How much money did they collect? _____

MULTIPLICATION

Name _____

Circle the correct answer.

1. $4{,}260 \times 7 = 29{,}820$

In this problem, 29,820 is _____.
a. the product   **b.** a factor   **c.** the divisor

2. $3 \times 1{,}795 = \boxed{}$

In this problem, the product is _____.
a. 3   **b.** 1,795   **c.** missing

3. $7{,}613 \times 2 = \boxed{}$

In this problem, 2 is _____.
a. a factor   **b.** the product   **c.** an answer

4. $1 \times 2{,}947 = 2{,}947$

In this problem, 1 is a _____.
a. factor   **b.** product   **c.** addend

5. $2 \times 777 = 1{,}554$

In this problem, 2 and 777 are _____.
a. factors   **b.** the product   **c.** the divisors

MULTIPLICATION

Name _____

Fill in the blanks with words from the box. You can use a word more than once.

multiply	factors	product

1. $5{,}278 \times 8 = \boxed{}$

To solve this problem, you must _____ the factors.

2. When you multiply the factors, the answer is called the _____.

3. $8 \times 4{,}033 = 32{,}264$

In this number sentence, 8 and 4,033 are the _____.

4. The order of the _____ does not change the product.

MULTIPLICATION

Name _____

Every year, Central School holds the Great Domino Challenge to raise money for charity. In the challenge, players set up their dominos so they fall one after another. Each player must use 4,848 dominos. There are 8 players. How many dominos are used in the challenge?

1. Which piece of information do you *not* need to answer the question? Circle the correct answer.

    a. the number of players

    b. the name of the domino challenge

    c. the number of dominos that each player uses

2. Which operation should you use to find the product? Circle the correct answer.

    a. addition

    b. subtraction

    c. multiplication

3. Each player uses _____ dominos.

4. There are _____ players in the Great Domino Challenge.

5. In this problem, _____ and _____ are the factors.

6. There will be _____ dominos used in the challenge.

MULTIPLICATION

Name _____

A. Find each product.

1. $3 \times 4 =$ _____

2. $57 \times 5 =$ _____

3. $604 \times 5 =$ _____

4.
$$\begin{array}{r} 834 \\ \times\ \ \ 8 \\ \hline \end{array}$$

5.
$$\begin{array}{r} 2{,}074 \\ \times\ \ \ \ \ 7 \\ \hline \end{array}$$

B. Unscramble the multiplication words.

1. t u l m p i l y _____

2. o r p c t u d _____

3. t o r f a c _____

C. Find which baseball card collection is better!

Jules collects baseball cards. At a flea market he sees two boxes of old cards for sale. Box A has 6 bundles of cards, and each bundle has 125 cards. Box B has 3 bundles of cards. Each of those bundles has 450 cards. Both boxes are the same price. Jules wants the box with the most cards. Which one should he buy?

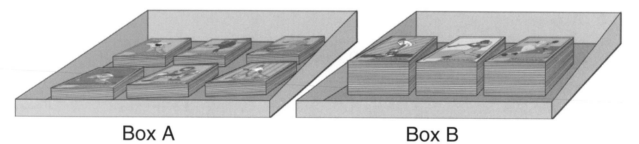

Box A   Box B

1. How many cards are in Box A? _____

2. How many cards are in Box B? _____

3. Which box of baseball cards should Jules buy? _____

DIVISION

Name _____

Divide.

1. $36 \div 4 =$ _____

2. $56 \div 7 =$ _____

3. $18 \div 3 =$ _____

4. $54 \div 6 =$ _____

5. $35 \div 5 =$ _____

DIVISION

Name _____

Solve by dividing.

1. There are 21 students in the class. The teacher divides the students into 7 equal groups. How many students are in each group? _____

2. Jose has 64 crayons. He has 8 friends. He wants to give each friend the same number of crayons. How many crayons does he give to each friend? _____

3. There are 4 runners on the long-distance relay team. They ran a 12-mile race. Each runner ran the same distance. How many miles did each runner run? _____

DIVISION

WEEK
DAY
3
THIRTEEN

Name _____

Fill in the blanks with words from the box. Use each word twice.

divisor	dividend	quotient

1. In 8 ÷ 4 = 2, the number 8 is the _____.

2. In 8 ÷ 4 = 2, the number 4 is the _____.

3. In 8 ÷ 4 = 2, the number 2 is the _____.

4. In 50 ÷ 5 = 10, the number 50 is the _____.

5. In 50 ÷ 5 = 10, the number 5 is the _____.

6. In 50 ÷ 5 = 10, the number 10 is the _____.

DIVISION

WEEK
DAY
4
THIRTEEN

Name _____

Fill in the table with the correct numbers.

	Divisor	Dividend	Quotient
1. 12 ÷ 2 = 6			
2. 42 ÷ 7 = 6			
3. 16 ÷ 1 = 16			
4. 40 ÷ 8 = 5			
5. 14 ÷ 7 = 2			

DIVISION

Name _____

Max and Tommy are going to a baseball card show. They each hope to make a lot of money selling baseball cards. Max has 54 baseball cards he wants to sell. Tommy has 42 cards he wants to sell. The two boys each decide to put their baseball cards into packs of 6 cards. How many packs will each boy have?

1. Max has _____ baseball cards.

2. Tommy has _____ baseball cards.

3. Max and Tommy both want to divide their cards into packs of _____.

4. Which operation should you use to find out how many packs of cards Max and Tommy have? Circle the correct answer.

    a. subtraction   **b.** division   **c.** multiplication

5. To find out how many packs Max will have, you must _____ _____ by _____.

6. To find out how many packs Tommy will have, you must _____ _____ by _____.

7. Max will have _____ packs of 6 baseball cards each.

8. Tommy will have _____ packs of 6 baseball cards each.

9. Set up a subtraction problem to find how many more packs Max has than Tommy. Then, solve.

_____

_____

DIVISION

Name _____

Solve.

1. $7\overline{)406}$

2. $5\overline{)115}$

3. $4\overline{)268}$

4. $728 \div 1 =$ _____

5. $198 \div 3 =$ _____

DIVISION

Name _____

Solve by dividing.

1. There are 204 people going to the football game. They fill 6 buses. The same number of people is on each bus. How many people are on each bus? _____

2. A farmer collected 574 eggs. Each hen laid exactly 7 eggs. How many hens are there? _____

3. Miguel earned $612 at his job. He makes $9 an hour. How many hours did he work? _____

4. A clothing factory has 430 yards of cloth. It takes 5 yards of cloth to make a suit. How many suits can the factory make? _____

DIVISION

Name _____

Complete the sentences to show how to estimate.

1. Juan wants to estimate the quotient of 212 divided by 4. He rounds

   212 to _____ so that 4 divides it easily. Then, he knows the
   quotient is about 50.

2. Roberta wants to estimate the quotient of 366 divided by 6. He knows

   that 6 goes into 36 evenly. So he rounds 366 to _____ so he finds
   an estimate of 60 easily.

3. Becky wants to estimate the quotient of 198 divided by 9. First, she

   rounds 198 to 200. Then she rounds 9 to _____. She estimates
   the quotient is about 20.

© Weekly Reader Corporation

DIVISION

Name _____

Fill in the table with the correct numbers.

	Divisor	Dividend	Quotient
1. $196 \div 2 = 98$			
2. $609 \div 7 = 87$			
3. $220 \div 4 = 55$			
4. $6\overline{)144}$ with quotient 24			
5. $3\overline{)195}$ with quotient 65			

© Weekly Reader Corporation

DIVISION

Name _____

Mr. Seabrook owns a juice bar. He needs to increase the speed that he can make orange juice. To do that, he needs to buy a new orange juice machine. He can afford two different machines. The Model ZK cuts and squeezes the juice from 380 oranges in 4 hours. The Model XB cuts and squeezes the juice from 455 oranges in 5 hours. Which machine squeezes more oranges in one hour?

1. Model ZK squeezes _____ oranges in _____ hours.

2. Model XB squeezes _____ oranges in _____ hours.

3. Which operation can you use to find out how many oranges each machine can squeeze in one hour? Circle the correct answer.

    a. multiplication   **b.** division   **c.** addition

4. To find the rate per hour of Model ZK, you must _____ _____ by _____.

5. To find the rate per hour of Model XB, you must _____ _____ by _____.

6. Model ZK squeezes _____ oranges per hour.

7. Model XB squeezes _____ oranges per hour.

8. Which model is faster? Circle the correct answer.

    a. Model ZK   **b.** Model XB

DIVISION

WEEK FIFTEEN · DAY 1

Name _____

Solve by dividing.

1. If 6 baseballs cost $24, how much does each baseball cost? _____

2. A bundle of 8 magazines costs $40. How much is each magazine? _____

3. At the science museum, 3 students each bought the same book. Together they spent $111. How much did each book cost? _____

4. After her party, Mary bought 9 thank-you cards for her guests. The cards were the same, and they cost $18 altogether. How much did she spend on each card? _____

Daily Math Practice

DIVISION

WEEK FIFTEEN · DAY 2

Name _____

Solve.

1. A box of 8 pairs of jeans costs $384. How much does each pair of jeans cost? _____

2. A shipment of 4 DVD players costs $212. How much does each DVD player cost? _____

3. The baseball coach bought 7 new bats. Each bat costs the same, and altogether he spent $301. How much did he pay for each bat? _____

4. Mr. Miller bought a set of 6 chairs for $408. How much did he pay for each chair? _____

DIVISION

Name _____

Estimate the cost of each item.

1. Pete bought 9 lampshades for $207. About how much did each lampshade cost?

    _____

2. The bike store bought 8 pairs of bike shorts. The store paid $410 for the shorts. What was the price of one pair of bike shorts?

    _____

3. Mrs. Strong bought 3 beach towels for $91. About how much did she pay for each towel?

    _____

4. It costs $688 to buy 8 new skateboards. If each skateboard cost the same amount, what is the price of each skateboard?

    _____

DIVISION

Name _____

Fill in the blanks with the words from the box. Use each word once.

| price | glove | total | each |

1. Three baseball gloves cost a total of $141. Each _____ costs $47.

2. Johnny bought 9 costumes for $567. The _____ of each costume was $63.

3. Frank bought 6 pounds of swordfish. The _____ cost was $102, so the price per pound was $17.

4. For the class party, the teacher bought 5 pizzas for $65. The pizzas cost $13 _____.

DIVISION

Name _____

Susie wants to paint her bedroom. She wants to use either yellow paint or blue paint. The paint store is having a sale. Susie decides to buy the paint that costs less per gallon. Which color should she buy?

PAINT SALE
Yellow 3 gallons $96
Blue 4 gallons $108

1. What is the total cost of 3 gallons of yellow paint? _____

2. Which operation should you use to find the price of one gallon of yellow paint? _____

3. Set up a problem to find the cost per gallon of yellow paint. Then, solve. _____

4. What is the total cost of 4 gallons blue paint? _____

5. Which operation should you use to find the price of one gallon of blue paint? _____

6. Set up a problem to find the cost per gallon of blue paint. Then, solve. _____

7. Which color paint is cheaper per gallon?

_____

DIVISION

Name _____

Find the missing number in each equation.

1. $32 \div \boxed{} = 8$

$\boxed{} = $ _____

2. $8 \times \boxed{} = 56$

$\boxed{} = $ _____

3. $\boxed{} \times 5 = 45$

$\boxed{} = $ _____

4. $49 \div \boxed{} = 49$

$\boxed{} = $ _____

DIVISION

Name _____

Find the missing number in each equation.

1. $\boxed{} \div 9 = 657$

$\boxed{} = $ _____

2. $\boxed{} \div 2 = 431$

$\boxed{} = $ _____

3. $5 \times \boxed{} = 230$

$\boxed{} = $ _____

4. $3 \times \boxed{} = 153$

$\boxed{} = $ _____

DIVISION

Name _____

Solve. Then, fill in each blank.

1. $1 \times \boxed{} = 41$ In this equation, the missing factor is _____.

2. $8 \times \boxed{} = 480$ In this equation, the missing factor is _____.

3. $\boxed{} \times 5 = 905$ In this equation, the missing factor is _____.

4. $\boxed{} \times 78 = 0$ In this equation, the missing factor is _____.

5. $2 \times \boxed{} = 532$ In this equation, the missing _____ is _____.

DIVISION

Name _____

Solve. Then, fill in each blank.

1. $\boxed{} \div 6 = 5$ In this equation, the missing dividend is _____.

2. $\boxed{} \div 4 = 77$ In this equation, the missing dividend is _____.

3. $126 \div \boxed{} = 14$ In this equation, the missing divisor is _____.

4. $577 \div \boxed{} = 577$ In this equation, the missing _____ is _____.

5. $\boxed{} \div 2 = 450$ In this equation, the missing _____ is _____.

DIVISION

Name _____

Mr. Johnston took his science class to see a movie. Mr. Johnston paid for the tickets using money from the class treasury. The tickets were $8 each. Mr. Johnston paid $240 for all the tickets, including his own. How many tickets did he buy?

1. The tickets to the movie cost $_____ each.

2. The total cost for all the tickets was $_____.

3. This problem can be solved using multiplication. Fill in the missing numbers.

$$\$\underline{\hspace{2cm}} \times \boxed{} = \$\underline{\hspace{2cm}}$$

4. To solve this multiplication problem, you can rewrite it using which operation? Circle the correct answer.

   a. addition   **b.** subtraction   **c.** division

5. Which expression will help you find how many tickets Mr. Johnston bought? Circle the correct answer.

   a. $240 ÷ 8   **b.** $240 × 8   **c.** $240 ÷ 240

6. Mr. Johnston bought _____ tickets.

MONTH
Review
FOUR

DIVISION

Name _____

A. Find each quotient.

1. $45 \div 5 =$ _____

2. $7\overline{)637}$

3. $6\overline{)894}$

B. Find the missing factor, dividend, or divisor.

1. $4 \times \boxed{} = 36$ The missing factor is _____.

2. $64 \div \boxed{} = 8$ The missing divisor is _____.

3. $\boxed{} \div 8 = 3$ The missing dividend is _____.

C. Solve the riddle.

Find each missing factor. Then, use the numbers to find the matching letters. The letters will spell the answer to this riddle. The first one is done.

Riddle: *What goes up when the rain comes down?*

1. $\boxed{8} \times 4 = 32$ (A)   2. $\boxed{} \times 7 = 21$ (B)

3. $\boxed{} \times 9 = 63$ (L)   4. $\boxed{} \times 4 = 4$ (U)

5. $\boxed{} \times 3 = 27$ (S)   6. $\boxed{} \times 5 = 30$ (L)

7. $\boxed{} \times 8 = 16$ (M)   8. $\boxed{} \times 8 = 32$ (R)

9. $\boxed{} \times 7 = 35$ (E)

$$\underset{1}{\rule{1cm}{0.4pt}} \quad \underset{2}{\rule{1cm}{0.4pt}} \quad \underset{3}{\rule{1cm}{0.4pt}} \quad \underset{4}{\rule{1cm}{0.4pt}} \quad \underset{5}{\rule{1cm}{0.4pt}} \quad \underset{6}{\rule{1cm}{0.4pt}} \quad \underset{7}{\rule{1cm}{0.4pt}} \quad \overset{A}{\underset{8}{\rule{1cm}{0.4pt}}} \quad \underset{9}{\rule{1cm}{0.4pt}}$$

GEOMETRY

Name _____

Match the shape on the left to its name on the right.

1.   triangle

2.   hexagon

3.   rectangle

4.   pentagon

5.   quadrilateral

GEOMETRY

Name _____

Write the name of each polygon. Use each name in the box only once.

| pentagon | square | octagon | quadrilateral | hexagon |

1.   _____

2.   _____

3.   _____

4.   _____

5.   _____

GEOMETRY

Name _____

The first letters in a word can tell you what the word means. Look at the names of the different polygons. Circle the correct answer.

1. *Quad–* in *quadrilateral* means _____.
   a. five   **b.** six   **c.** four

2. *Octa–* in *octagon* means _____.
   a. six   **b.** eight   **c.** seven

3. *Tri–* in *triangle* means _____.
   a. five   **b.** three   **c.** four

4. *Penta–* in *pentagon* means _____.
   a. six   **b.** four   **c.** five

5. *Hexa–* in *hexagon* means _____.
   a. six   **b.** seven   **c.** three

GEOMETRY

Name _____

Write the number of sides and vertices for each polygon.

1. All rectangles and squares have _____ sides and _____ vertices.

2. Octagons have _____ sides and _____ vertices.

3. Hexagons have _____ sides and _____ vertices.

4. Pentagons have _____ sides and _____ vertices.

5. Triangles have _____ sides and _____ vertices.

GEOMETRY

Name _____

Juanita's room is in the shape of the letter "L." She draws the floor plan using two rectangles.

I. Draw the shape of Juanita's room in the space below.

2. How many sides does your figure have? _____

3. How many walls does Juanita's room have? _____

4. Juanita buys a table for her room. It is in the shape of a quadrilateral. However, it is not in the shape of a square or a rectangle. Draw a quadrilateral that is not a square or a rectangle.

5. How many vertices does the table have? _____

6. How many sides does the table have? _____

GEOMETRY

Name _____

Match the congruent shapes.

1. ◿

a. ▱

2. ☐

b. ◁

3. △

c. ⬖

4. ▭

d. ◇

5. ⬠

e. ◺

GEOMETRY

Name _____

Is each pair of figures congruent? Write *yes* or *no*.

1. ☐   ▭   _____

2. ◿   ◿   _____

3. ⬠   ⬠   _____

4. ⬠   ⬡   _____

5. ⬢   ⬡   _____

GEOMETRY

Name _____

Fill in the blanks with words from the box. Use each word once.

congruent	similar	shape	size	square

1. Figures that have the same shape but are not the same size
are _____.

2. Figures that have exactly the same size and shape are _____.

3. A triangle and a _____ cannot be congruent or similar.

4. Two rectangles can be congruent if they have the same shape
and _____.

5. Two triangles that have the same _____ but are different sizes
are similar.

GEOMETRY

Name _____

Fill in each blank. Use the words *similar* or *congruent*.

1. These pentagons are the same
shape and size. They are _____.

2. These hexagons are the same shape
but different sizes. They are _____.

Draw the figures.

3. Draw two congruent squares.

GEOMETRY

Name _____

The Hong family is building a house. Their twin boys are getting separate rooms. They want to have rooms that are exactly the same size and shape. That means the rooms have to be congruent.

The first drawings for the two rooms are below.

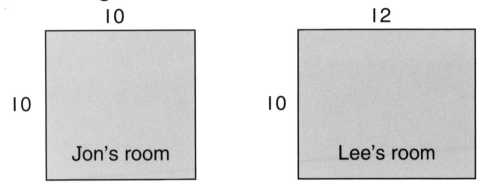

Use the Hong family's plans to answer the questions. Circle the correct answer.

1. The drawings of Jon's room and Lee's room are
   a. congruent.
   b. similar.
   c. not congruent nor similar.

2. How could the Hong family change Jon's room to make it congruent with Lee's room?
   a. Change the dimensions to 12 by 12.
   b. Change the dimensions to 10 by 10.
   c. Change the dimensions to 12 by 10.

3. How could the Hong family change Lee's room to make it congruent with Jon's room?
   a. Change the dimensions to 12 by 12.
   b. Change the dimensions to 10 by 10.
   c. Change the dimensions to 10 by 12.

4. Jon and Lee decide they want larger rooms in the shape of squares. Is it possible for the shapes *not* to be similar? Explain your answer.

_____

_____

GEOMETRY

Name _____

Is the dotted line a line of symmetry? Write *yes* or *no*.

1. _____

2. _____

3.  _____

4. _____

5. _____

GEOMETRY

Name _____

Draw a line of symmetry for each shape.

1.

2.

3.

4.

GEOMETRY

Name _____

Some shapes have more than one line of symmetry. Draw as many as you can. Write how many you found.

1. _____

2.  _____

3. _____

4. _____

5. _____

GEOMETRY

Name _____

Circle *true* or *false*.

1. If a line divides a figure into two congruent parts, it is a line of symmetry.

   true   false

2. All shapes can be divided by a line of symmetry.

   true   false

3. Some shapes can be divided by more than one line of symmetry.

   true   false

4. A circle has exactly four lines of symmetry.

   true   false

GEOMETRY

Name _____

Each dotted line is a line of symmetry. Complete each figure.

1.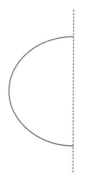

2.

3.

4.

5.

GEOMETRY

Name _____

Match the solid shape with its name.

1.   **a.** cylinder

2.   **b.** sphere

3.   **c.** cube

4.   **d.** rectangular pyramid

5.   **e.** cone

GEOMETRY

Name _____

Fill in each blank.

1. A cube has _____ flat sides.

2. A rectangular prism has _____ vertices.

3. A cylinder has _____ flat sides.

4. A rectangular pyramid has _____ flat sides and _____ vertices.

5. A cone has _____ flat side(s).

GEOMETRY

Name _____

Fill in the blanks with words from the box. Use each word once.

face	vertex	vertices	edge	prism

1. Another name for a side of a solid is _____.

2. Another name for a corner of a solid is _____.

3. The line created when two faces meet is called an _____.

4. A cube has more than one vertex. It has 8 _____.

5. A rectangular solid is also called a rectangular _____.

GEOMETRY

Name _____

Name each solid. Use the drawings to help.

cube **rectangular solid** **cone** **cylinder** **square pyramid**

1. I have 2 faces that are circles. _____

2. I have 5 faces and 8 edges. _____

3. I have 12 edges that are all the same length. _____

4. I have 1 flat face and 1 vertex. _____

5. I have 12 edges that can be 3 different sizes. _____

GEOMETRY

Name _____

How does each solid shape look from the side? Circle the correct answer.

1.   a.   b.   c.

2. 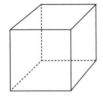   a.   b.    c.

3. 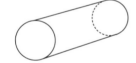   a.   b.    c.

4.    a.    b.   c.

5. 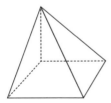   a.   b.   c.

GEOMETRY

MONTH
Review
FIVE

Name _____

A. Fill in the blanks with names from the box. Use each name once.

| pentagon   cube   quadrilateral   hexagon |

1. _____

2. _____

3. _____

4. _____

B. Draw a line of symmetry for each shape. If possible, draw more than one line of symmetry.

1.

2.

3.

C. Find the shapes at the park.

Samantha is on a treasure hunt at the park. She is looking for the shapes on her list. Circle each shape when you find it.

| cube   sphere   cylinder   cone |

MEASUREMENT

Name _____

Measure each length in centimeters.

1. 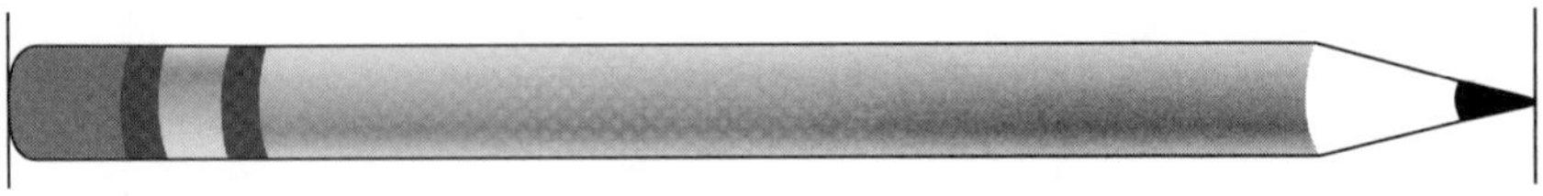 _____ centimeters

2. 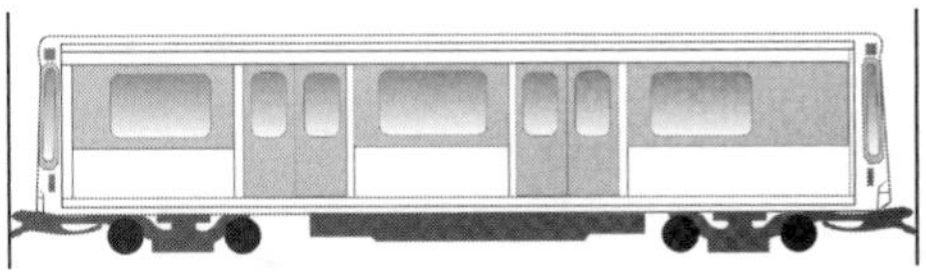 _____ centimeters

3. 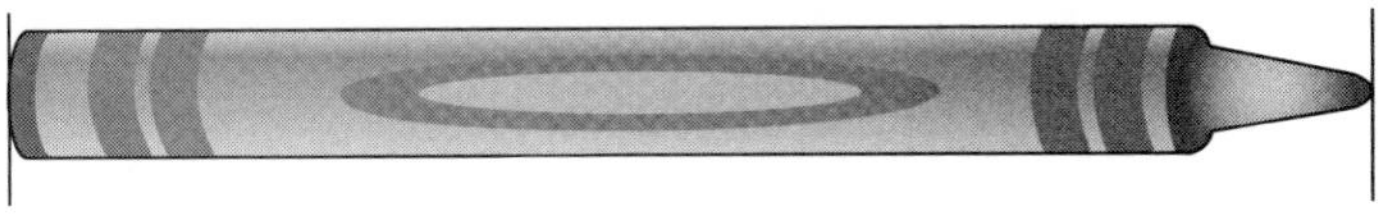 _____ centimeters

4. 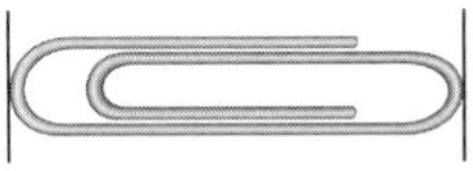 _____ centimeters

5. 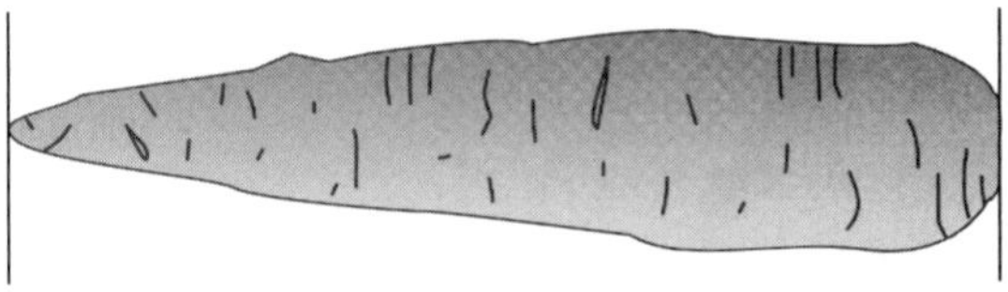 _____ centimeters

© Weekly Reader Corporation

MEASUREMENT

Name _____

Measure each length in inches.

1. 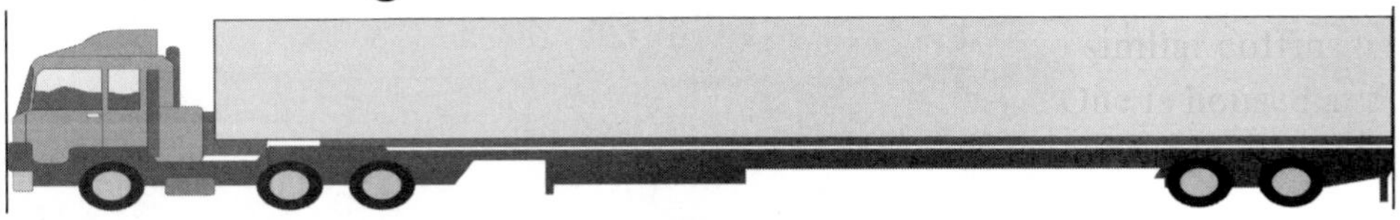 _____ inches

2.  _____ inches

3.  _____ inches

4. 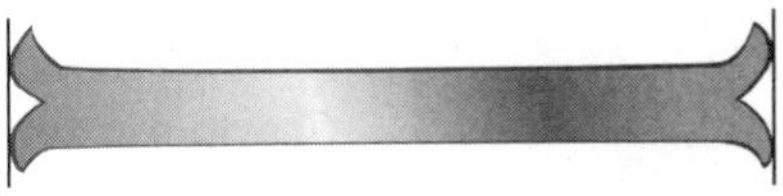 _____ inches

5. 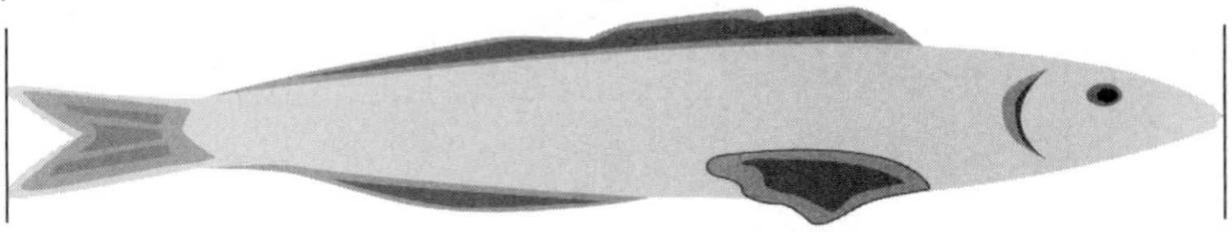 _____ inches

© Weekly Reader Corporation

MEASUREMENT

WEEK TWENTY ONE
DAY 3

Name _____

Compare the measurements. Fill in the blanks with words from the box. Use each word once.

length	centimeters	feet	inches	longer

1. Jack has a train that is 34 centimeters long. Sarah has a train that is 38 centimeters long. Sarah's train is _____.

2. A bed is about 6 _____ long.

3. The _____ of Mr. Peters's shoe is about 12 inches.

4. There are 100 _____ in a meter.

5. There are 12 _____ in a foot.

MEASUREMENT

WEEK TWENTY ONE
DAY 4

Name _____

Match the unit of measure with its abbreviation.

1. cm   **a.** yard

2. in.   **b.** meter

3. yd   **c.** feet

4. ft   **d.** centimeter

5. m   **e.** inch

MEASUREMENT

Name _____

Owen wants to order his items from shortest to longest. Help Owen measure each object in inches. Then, put them in order.

bookmark: _____ inches

paper clip: _____ inches

race car: _____ inches

key: _____ inches

pen: _____ inches

thumbtack: _____ inches

Write the names of the objects in order from shortest to longest.

_____

_____

MEASUREMENT

Name _____

Find the perimeter of each rectangle.

1.

7 ft

3 ft ☐ 3 ft

7 ft

_____

2.

8 in.

1 in. ☐ 1 in.

8 in.

_____

3.

3 ft

4 ft ☐ 4 ft

3 ft

_____

4.

5 yd

2 yd ☐ 2 yd

5 yd

_____

MEASUREMENT

Name _____

Find the perimeter of each rectangle.

1.

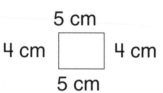

5 cm

4 cm ☐ 4 cm

5 cm

_____

2.

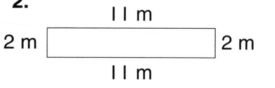

11 m

2 m ☐ 2 m

11 m

_____

3.

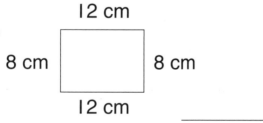

12 cm

8 cm ☐ 8 cm

12 cm

_____

4.

9 m

3 m ☐ 3 m

9 m

_____

MEASUREMENT

Name _____

Compare the measurements. Fill in the blanks with words from the box. Use each word once.

| perimeter | sides | length | multiply | add |

1. The distance around a figure is called its _____.

2. Perimeters are measured in units of _____.

3. To find the perimeter of a polygon, you can add the length of its
   _____.

4. To find the perimeter of a square, you can _____
   the length of one side by 4.

5. To find the perimeter of a rectangle, you can _____
   the lengths of its sides.

© Weekly Reader Corporation

MEASUREMENT

Name _____

Find each perimeter.

1. A rectangular swimming pool measures 50 meters by 30 meters.

   What is the perimeter of the pool? _____ meters

2. The Greenbergs have a big deck. The deck is a rectangle 35 feet by

   45 feet. What is the perimeter of the deck? _____ feet

3. Mary's square kitchen table is 30 inches on each side. What is its

   perimeter? _____ inches

4. A rancher has a rectangular corral that is 40 yards long and 25 yards wide.

   What is the perimeter of the corral? _____ yards

© Weekly Reader Corporation

MEASUREMENT

Name _____

Maria bought a picture frame for a present. She will put her picture in the frame. Then she will give it to her parents. She wants to decorate the frame with ribbon. To find out how much ribbon she needs, she must find the perimeter of the frame. Help Maria find her perimeter. Use your ruler.

1. What is the length of the top side of Maria's picture frame?

   _____

2. What is the length of the right side of Maria's picture frame?

   _____

3. What is the length of the bottom side of Maria's picture frame?

   _____

4. What is the length of the left side of Maria's picture frame?

   _____

5. Which operation should you use to find the perimeter of the frame? Circle the correct answer.

   a. subtraction   **b.** addition   **c.** multiplication

6. Write an expression that shows how you can find the perimeter.

   _____

7. What is the perimeter of Maria's picture frame? _____ inches

8. How much ribbon will Maria need? _____ inches

MEASUREMENT

Name _____

Count the units. Find the area for each shape.

1. 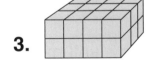 _____ square units

2.  _____ square units

3. _____ square units

4. _____ square units

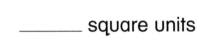

5. _____ square units

MEASUREMENT

Name _____

Count the cubes. Find the volume for each solid.

1. _____ cubic units

2. _____ cubic units

3. _____ cubic units

4. _____ cubic units

MEASUREMENT

Name _____

Fill in the blanks with words from the box. Use each word once.

polygon	perimeter	area	volume	solid

1. The amount of space that fills a solid is the _____.

2. The distance around a figure is its _____.

3. The amount of space that will cover a figure is its _____.

4. A _____ has length, width, and depth.

5. A _____ is a figure made up of straight lines.

MEASUREMENT

Name _____

Circle whether you would find the area or the volume of each figure.

1.   area   volume

2.    area   volume

3. 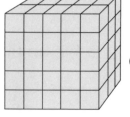   area   volume

4. 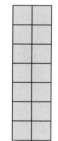   area   volume

MEASUREMENT

Name _____

Kenny wants to measure the area and perimeter of the figure below. Help him find his answers.

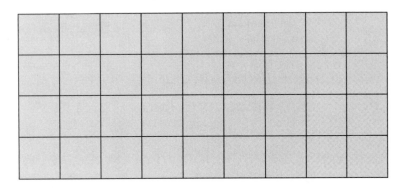

1. How many units are in the top row? _____

2. How many rows are in the figure? _____

3. How can you use the answers from questions 1 and 2 to find the area of the figure? Circle the correct answer.

    a. Add them.   **b.** Multiply them.   **c.** Subtract them.

4. How else can you find the area of Kenny's figure? Circle the correct answer.

    a. Count the total number of units.

    b. Add the lengths of the 4 sides.

    c. Divide the perimeter by the sides.

5. What is the area of Kenny's figure? _____ square units

6. How can you find the perimeter of Kenny's figure? Circle the correct answer.

    a. Count the total number of units.

    b. Add the lengths of the 4 sides.

    c. Multiply the length of the figure by the width.

7. What is the perimeter of Kenny's figure? _____ units

MEASUREMENT

Name _____

Circle the correct answer.

1. What could you use to measure the weight of a package?

    a. a ruler   **b.** a scale   **c.** a measuring cup

2. What could you use to measure an amount of water?

    a. a yardstick   **b.** a measuring cup   **c.** a tape measure

3. What could you use to measure the length of a piece of wood?

    a. a tape measure   **b.** a scale   **c.** a measuring spoon

4. What could you use to draw a line exactly 5 inches long?

    a. a scale   **b.** a ruler   **c.** a measuring cup

© Weekly Reader Corporation

MEASUREMENT

Name _____

For each unit of measure, write whether it shows capacity, length, or weight.

1. liters   _____

2. meters   _____

3. inches   _____

4. pounds   _____

5. cups   _____

© Weekly Reader Corporation

80

MEASUREMENT

Name _____

Fill in the blanks with words from the box. Use each word once.

| weight | cup | gallon | pounds | scale |

Rebecca wanted to know how much she weighed. She stepped on a

_____. It said that she weighed 75 _____. She was thirsty.

So she went to the kitchen for some milk. She took a _____ of

milk from the fridge. Then she poured herself a _____. After she

drank it, she wondered if her _____ was higher!

MEASUREMENT

Name _____

Circle the word that completes each sentence.

1. At the supermarket, they measure meat in _____.
   a. pounds   **b.** gallons   **c.** yards

2. You can measure the amount of sugar in a box using _____.
   a. gallons   **b.** inches   **c.** cups

3. A gram is a unit of _____.
   a. mass   **b.** length   **c.** volume

4. You can measure weight using _____.
   a. cups   **b.** feet   **c.** ounces

5. You can measure the amount of juice in a bottle using _____.
   a. pounds   **b.** yards   **c.** liters

MEASUREMENT

Name _____

There are different systems of measure.
Sometimes you will use the customary
system. Sometimes you will use the
metric system. Look at each question.
Circle the best customary unit of
measure to use. Then, circle the best
metric unit of measure to use.

1. Springfield is planning a race from one end of the city to the other.
   Which unit of measure should they use for the distance of their race?

   Customary: inches   ounces   gallons   miles

   Metric: meters   grams   kilometers   liters

2. Ms. Rodriguez drives her car to the gas station. Which unit of measure
   should she use to measure the amount of gas she puts in her car?

   Customary: feet   ounces   gallons   miles

   Metric: meters   grams   kilograms   liters

3. A grocery store sells bananas. The cost of the bananas is based on
   their weight or mass. Which unit of measure should the store use to
   measure the weight or mass of the bananas?

   Customary: pounds   cups   yards   gallons

   Metric: meters   kilograms   kilometers   liters

4. A baker wants to bake a cake. Which unit of measure should he use to
   measure the amount of milk he needs to bake the cake?

   Customary: gallons   inches   cups   pounds

   Metric: centimeters   kilograms   meters   liters

MEASUREMENT

Name _____

A. Find each perimeter.

1. A square has sides that are 6 meters long.
   What is its perimeter?   _____ meters

2. Rose's garden is in the shape of a rectangle. It has
   sides that are 15 yards, 15 yards, 11 yards, and
   11 yards. What is the perimeter of the garden?   _____ yards

3. Tom wants to make a frame for a painting.
   The frame is a 2-foot square. What is its perimeter? _____ feet

B. Circle the correct answer to complete each sentence.

1. You would most likely measure the mass of a dog in _____.

   a. kilograms   **b.** inches   **c.** centimeters

2. You would most likely weigh a refrigerator in _____.

   a. ounces   **b.** inches   **c.** pounds

3. You would most likely measure the weight of a letter in _____.

   a. tons   **b.** ounces   **c.** inches

**C. Find the units of measurement in the word search. Look up,
down, diagonally, forward, and backward. Circle each word
from the box below.**

cup	foot	gallon	gram	inch	meter
ounce	pound	quart	yard		

G	A	L	L	O	N	A	Q	U
R	R	Y	R	A	M	P	U	C
H	I	A	R	G	X	Q	A	A
C	N	R	M	E	T	E	R	N
N	P	D	N	U	O	P	T	A
I	E	C	N	U	O	A	O	F
Q	I	N	T	H	F	U	Z	O

FRACTIONS

Name _____

Match the fractions that have the same value.

1.   a.

2.   b.

3.    c.

4.   d.

5.    e.

FRACTIONS

Name _____

Shade each figure on the right to show an equivalent fraction.

1.

2.

3.

4.

FRACTIONS

Name _____

Fill in the blanks with words from the box. Use each word once.

denominator   numerator   equivalent   fraction

1. You can show parts of a whole or a group using a _____.

2. The _____ tells you the total number of equal parts in the whole or group.

3. The _____ tells you how many equal parts you are talking about.

4. Two fractions that are equal are called _____.

FRACTIONS

Name _____

Circle the correct answer.

1. Which fraction is equivalent to $\frac{1}{4}$?

   a. $\frac{1}{8}$ **b.** $\frac{2}{8}$ **c.** $\frac{2}{4}$

2. Which is the denominator in $\frac{5}{10}$?

   a. 5   **b.** 10   **c.** 15

3. An egg carton holds 6 eggs. There are 2 eggs in it. Which fraction shows how much of the carton is filled with eggs?

   a. $\frac{2}{4}$ **b.** $\frac{2}{6}$ **c.** $\frac{6}{2}$

4. Which is the numerator in $\frac{3}{5}$?

   a. 3   **b.** 5   **c.** 8

FRACTIONS

Name _____

Mr. Burns bought 10 colored pencils for his children, Henry and Marie. Henry got half of his father's pencils. Marie got four pencils from her father. Who got more pencils?

1. Color or shade the pencils below to show the pencils Henry got.

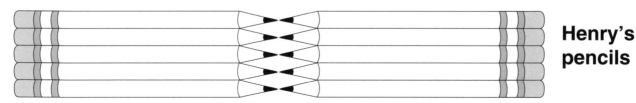

Henry's pencils

2. Write the amount of Henry's pencils as a fraction.   Henry: _____

3. Color or shade the pencils below to show the pencils Marie got.

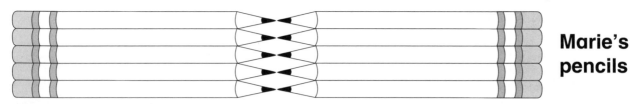

Marie's pencils

4. Write the amount of Marie's pencils as a fraction. Marie: _____

5. Are the fractions of Marie's and Henry's pencils equivalent? Explain why or why not.

_____

_____

6. Who had more pencils? _____

7. How many pencils should Marie get to make their shares equal?

_____

8. Write their equal shares as equivalent fractions. _____

FRACTIONS

Name _____

Add to find each sum.

1. $\frac{3}{8} + \frac{1}{8}$ = _____

2. $\frac{1}{4} + \frac{2}{4}$ = _____

3. $\frac{1}{6} + \frac{3}{6}$ = _____

4. $\frac{1}{5} + \frac{3}{5}$ = _____

5. $\frac{3}{10} + \frac{1}{10}$ = _____

FRACTIONS

Name _____

Add to find each sum.

1. $\frac{3}{8} + \frac{4}{8}$ = _____

2. $\frac{2}{6} + \frac{2}{6}$ = _____

3. $\frac{2}{8} + \frac{3}{8}$ = _____

4. $\frac{2}{5} + \frac{2}{5}$ = _____

5. $\frac{3}{10} + \frac{5}{10}$ = _____

FRACTIONS

Name _____

Circle the correct answer.

1. What is the denominator in $\frac{2}{6}$?

    a. 2   **b.** 6   **c.** $\frac{1}{4}$

2. What is the new fraction if you increased the numerator in $\frac{3}{8}$ by 1?

    a. $\frac{4}{8}$ **b.** $\frac{3}{9}$ **c.** $\frac{4}{9}$

3. Which is true about equivalent fractions?
    a. They must have the same denominator.
    b. They must have the same numerator.
    c. They must have the same value.

4. What are fractions that have the same denominator?
    a. like fractions   **b.** equal fractions   **c.** equivalent fractions

---

FRACTIONS

Name _____

Fill in the blanks with words from the box. Use each word once.

| like | plus | add | denominator | numerator |

1. When you _____ $\frac{1}{3}$ and $\frac{1}{3}$, the sum is $\frac{2}{3}$.

2. $\frac{7}{10}$ _____ $\frac{2}{10}$ equals $\frac{9}{10}$.

3. $\frac{6}{8}$ and $\frac{1}{8}$ are examples of _____ fractions.

4. Like fractions have the same _____.

5. You add like fractions by adding the _____ together.

FRACTIONS

Name _____

Luis bought a gallon of paint to paint his room.
He used $\frac{1}{3}$ of the gallon on the first coat. Then he
used another $\frac{1}{3}$ of the gallon for a second coat.
Luis wants to find out how much paint he used
for both coats.

1. How much paint did Luis use for the first coat?_____ gallon

2. How much paint did Luis use for the second coat? _____ gallon

3. Which expression shows how much paint Luis used?
   Circle the correct answer.

   a. $\frac{1}{3} + \frac{1}{3}$ **b.** $\frac{1}{3} - \frac{1}{3}$ **c.** $\frac{1}{3} + \frac{2}{3}$

4. How much paint did Luis use in total? _____

Ten students from the Greenwood School visited a museum.
Teddy and Angela bought postcards. Taryn bought a book.
No one else bought anything. Taryn wants to figure out what
fraction of the students bought something on the trip.

5. How many students visited the museum? _____

6. How many students bought postcards? _____

7. What fraction of the students bought postcards? _____

8. How many students bought a book? _____

9. What fraction of the students bought a book? _____

10. Write an addition problem to show what fraction of the students
    bought something at the museum. Solve to find the total.

_____

FRACTIONS

Name _____

Circle the correct difference.

1. $\frac{2}{5} - \frac{1}{5} = \boxed{}$ **a.** $\frac{3}{5}$ **b.** $\frac{3}{10}$ **c.** $\frac{1}{5}$

2. $\frac{5}{8} - \frac{1}{8} = \boxed{}$ **a.** $\frac{4}{8}$ **b.** $\frac{6}{8}$ **c.** $\frac{6}{16}$

3. $\frac{3}{10} - \frac{2}{10} = \boxed{}$ **a.** $\frac{10}{3}$ **b.** $\frac{1}{10}$ **c.** $\frac{5}{10}$

4. $\frac{5}{6} - \frac{2}{6} = \boxed{}$ **a.** $\frac{2}{6}$ **b.** $\frac{6}{3}$ **c.** $\frac{3}{6}$

5. $\frac{4}{4} - \frac{3}{4} = \boxed{}$ **a.** $\frac{7}{4}$ **b.** 1 **c.** $\frac{1}{4}$

FRACTIONS

Name _____

Subtract to find each difference.

1. $\frac{6}{8} - \frac{3}{8} =$ _____   2. $\frac{7}{10} - \frac{1}{10} =$ _____

3. $\frac{3}{4} - \frac{2}{4} =$ _____   4. $\frac{4}{5} - \frac{3}{5} =$ _____

5. $\frac{5}{6} - \frac{3}{6} =$ _____

FRACTIONS

Name _____

Circle the answer that completes each sentence.

1. To solve $\frac{4}{5} - \frac{3}{5}$, you must subtract the _____.

   a. numerators   **b.** denominators   **c.** sums

2. Like fractions must _____.

   a. be equal   **b.** have the same numerator   **c.** have the same denominator

3. If you _____ $\frac{4}{8}$ from $\frac{7}{8}$, the difference is $\frac{3}{8}$.

   a. add   **b.** subtract   **c.** multiply

4. The fractions $\frac{3}{5}$, $\frac{3}{8}$, and $\frac{3}{6}$ all have the same _____.

   a. numerator   **b.** denominator   **c.** numerator and denominator

---

FRACTIONS

Name _____

Fill in the blanks with words from the box. Use each word once.

denominator	minus	equivalent	difference

1. $\frac{2}{6}$ and $\frac{5}{6}$ have the same _____.

2. $\frac{3}{4}$ and $\frac{6}{8}$ have the same value, so they are _____.

3. $\frac{8}{10}$ _____ $\frac{3}{10}$ equals $\frac{5}{10}$.

4. When you subtract $\frac{2}{10}$ from $\frac{5}{10}$, the _____ is $\frac{3}{10}$.

FRACTIONS

Name _____

Mr. and Mrs. Monroe ordered a large pizza. The pizza was cut into 6 slices. Mr. Monroe ate 3 slices. Mrs. Monroe ate 2 slices. What fraction shows how much more of the pizza Mr. Monroe ate? Answer the questions to find out.

1. How many slices were in the whole pizza pie? _____

2. How many slices did Mr. Monroe eat? _____

3. Which fraction shows how much of the pie Mr. Monroe ate? _____

4. How many slices did Mrs. Monroe eat? _____

5. Which fraction shows how much of the pie Mrs. Monroe ate? _____

6. Write an equation using your fractions to show how much more pizza Mr. Monroe ate.

_____

7. Shade the fraction of the circle to show how much pizza Mr. Monroe ate. Use a pencil.

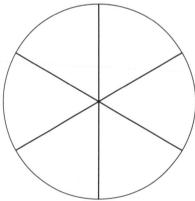

8. Use the figure above. Erase the shaded parts to show how much pizza Mrs. Monroe ate. What fraction does the shaded area that is left show? _____

FRACTIONS

Name _____

Use the number line. Fill in each ◯ using < or >.

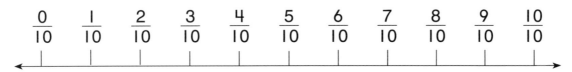

$$\frac{0}{10} \quad \frac{1}{10} \quad \frac{2}{10} \quad \frac{3}{10} \quad \frac{4}{10} \quad \frac{5}{10} \quad \frac{6}{10} \quad \frac{7}{10} \quad \frac{8}{10} \quad \frac{9}{10} \quad \frac{10}{10}$$

1. $\frac{1}{10}$ ◯ $\frac{6}{10}$

2. $\frac{7}{10}$ ◯ $\frac{4}{10}$

3. $\frac{5}{10}$ ◯ $\frac{9}{10}$

4. $\frac{2}{10}$ ◯ $\frac{3}{10}$

5. $\frac{10}{10}$ ◯ $\frac{8}{10}$

6. $\frac{6}{10}$ ◯ $\frac{5}{10}$

FRACTIONS

Name _____

Circle the greater fraction.

1. $\frac{3}{8}$ $\frac{4}{6}$

2. $\frac{1}{5}$ $\frac{1}{3}$

3. $\frac{2}{3}$ $\frac{3}{6}$

4. $\frac{2}{5}$ $\frac{3}{10}$

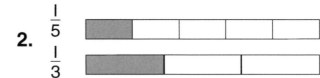

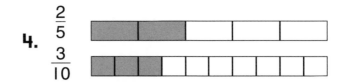

5. $\frac{7}{8}$ $\frac{5}{6}$

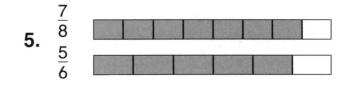

FRACTIONS

Name _____

Circle each correct answer.

1. Which is the numerator in the fraction $\frac{7}{8}$?

     a. 9   **b.** 8   **c.** 7

2. Which is correct?

     a. $\frac{2}{6} < \frac{2}{3}$ **b.** $\frac{1}{4} > \frac{2}{4}$ **c.** $\frac{1}{3} < \frac{2}{6}$

3. Which number is greater than $\frac{1}{2}$?

     a. $\frac{1}{3}$ **b.** $\frac{5}{10}$ **c.** $\frac{3}{4}$

4. Which number is less than $\frac{1}{2}$?

     a. $\frac{1}{3}$ **b.** $\frac{5}{10}$ **c.** 1

5. Which is the denominator in the fraction $\frac{4}{6}$?

     a. 4   **b.** 6   **c.** 10

FRACTIONS

Name _____

Fill in the blanks with words from the box. You can use words more than once.

less	greater	equals

1. The symbol > means is _____ than.

2. The symbol = means _____ .

3. The symbol < means _____ than.

4. The fraction $\frac{5}{6}$ is _____ than $\frac{7}{8}$.

5. The whole number 1 is _____ than $\frac{1}{10}$.

FRACTIONS

Name _____

Fill in each ◯ **using <, >, or =.**

1. A pint is $\frac{2}{4}$ of a quart. A cup is $\frac{1}{4}$ of a quart.

$\frac{2}{4}$ quart ◯ $\frac{1}{4}$ quart

2. John's lawn mower used $\frac{3}{5}$ gallon of gas in one hour. Eliza's mower used $\frac{4}{5}$ gallon in the same time.

$\frac{3}{5}$ gallon ◯ $\frac{4}{5}$ gallon

3. Meagan and Robert sold magazines to raise money. Both started with the same number of magazines. Meagan sold $\frac{7}{10}$ of her magazines. Robert sold $\frac{9}{10}$ of his magazines.

$\frac{7}{10}$ ◯ $\frac{9}{10}$

4. Two art classes started with equal stacks of paper. At the end of the month, Ms. Williams's class had used $\frac{2}{8}$ of their stack. Mr. Reardon's class had used $\frac{1}{4}$ of their paper.

$\frac{2}{8}$ ◯ $\frac{1}{4}$

5. Pete and Suzanne made costumes for the class play. Pete used $\frac{5}{6}$ yard of cloth. Suzanne used $\frac{4}{6}$ yard of cloth.

$\frac{5}{6}$ ◯ $\frac{4}{6}$

FRACTIONS

Name _____

A. Find each sum or difference.

1. $\frac{1}{8} + \frac{3}{8}$ = _____   **2.** $\frac{8}{10} - \frac{3}{10}$ = _____   **3.** $\frac{4}{6} + \frac{1}{6}$ = _____

B. Fill in the blanks with words from the box. Use each word once.

like   fractions   add   numerator   denominator

Judy mowed $\frac{3}{8}$ of her lawn on Saturday and $\frac{4}{8}$ on Sunday. To find

the total amount of the lawn she mowed, she needs to _____.

The fractions have the same _____, so they are _____.

That means she can add each _____ to find the total.

C. Solve the problems to answer the riddle. Find the letter for each answer in the box. Write it in the answer.

Riddle: *Where does a river keep its money?*

1. $\frac{3}{8} + \frac{2}{8}$ = _____   **2.** $\frac{10}{10} - \frac{5}{10}$ = _____   **3.** $\frac{5}{8} + \frac{2}{8}$ = _____

4. $\frac{3}{4} - \frac{1}{4}$ = _____   **5.** $\frac{2}{5} + \frac{1}{5}$ = _____   **6.** $\frac{3}{3} - \frac{2}{3}$ = _____

7. $\frac{2}{6} + \frac{3}{6}$ = _____   **8.** $\frac{9}{10} - \frac{2}{10}$ = _____

$\frac{5}{10}$ = T	$\frac{7}{8}$ = S	$\frac{5}{8}$ = I	$\frac{2}{4}$ = B
$\frac{5}{6}$ = K	$\frac{7}{10}$ = S	$\frac{3}{5}$ = A	$\frac{1}{3}$ = N

Answer: ____ ____ ____   ____ ____ ____ ____ ____
         1   2   3   4   5   6   7   8

GRAPHS, DATA, AND PROBABILITY

Name _____

Write whether each event is *certain, likely, unlikely,* or *impossible*.

1. Ms. Weinstein put 29 red marbles and one blue marble in a bag. Then she lets a student take one from the bag. It is _____ that a student will pick the blue marble.

2. Jane has 6 tickets to a concert. Each ticket is in the front row. Her friend closes her eyes and picks a ticket. It is _____ that her friend will get a front-row seat.

3. The coach is giving out jersey numbers to the soccer team. There are 25 numbers. Paula would like any number for her jersey except 7. It is _____ that Paula will get a number she likes.

GRAPHS, DATA, AND PROBABILITY

Name _____

Circle the number that makes the sentence true.

1. There are 24 guests at a party. There are 24 balloons, _____ of which are red. Each guest gets one balloon. It is likely that they will get a red balloon.
   a. 2   **b.** 10   **c.** 22

2. Rodrigo picks marbles out of a bag. There are 20 marbles in the bag. There are _____ green marbles. It is certain that he will pick a green marble.
   a. 0   **b.** 10   **c.** 20

3. Your teacher has a total of _____ cards. There are 9 red cards. It is likely that you will pick a red card.
   a. 2   **b.** 8   **c.** 10

GRAPHS, DATA, AND PROBABILITY

Name _____

Circle the term that tells about each event.

1. an event that will probably not happen
   a. likely   **b.** unlikely   **c.** equally likely

2. an event that will definitely happen
   a. likely   **b.** certain   **c.** impossible

3. an event that can never happen
   a. likely   **b.** unlikely   **c.** impossible

4. an event that will probably happen
   a. likely   **b.** unlikely   **c.** equally likely

5. an event that has the same chance of happening as of not happening
   a. equally likely   **b.** certain   **c.** impossible

GRAPHS, DATA, AND PROBABILITY

Name _____

Fill in each blank. Use the word *certain*, *likely*, *unlikely*, or *impossible*.

1. The weather forecaster thinks it will probably rain today. He thinks
   rain is _____.

2. The chance an event will happen is small, so it is _____.

3. The sun rises every morning. The chances of it rising on any day are
   _____.

4. About 1 out of 5 people are left-handed. It is _____ that
   a baby will be left-handed.

GRAPHS, DATA, AND PROBABILITY

Name _____

The students in Mr. Anastasio's class are playing a game. Each student writes a number from 1 to 5 on a card. They can use pen or pencil. There are 15 students in the class. After they write a number on the card, Mr. Anastasio mixes the cards. The numbers on the cards tell the players how many spaces they can move on a game board. The cards are shown below.

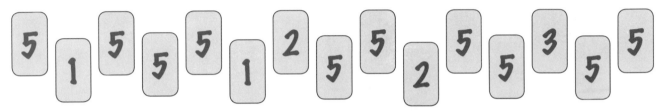

Sloan picks a card first. She wants to pick a 5.

1. There are _____ cards in all.

2. There are _____ cards with the number 5.

3. What chance does Sloan have of picking a 5?
   Circle the correct answer.
       a. unlikely   **b.** likely   **c.** certain

Jackson picks a card next. He wants to pick a 4.

4. There are _____ cards in all.

5. There are _____ cards with the number 4.

6. What chance does Jackson have of picking a 4?
   Circle the correct answer.
       a. impossible   **b.** likely   **c.** certain

7. Which information do you *not* need to find the probability of picking a 3?
   Circle the correct answer.
       a. There are 15 students in the class.
       b. The students used pen or pencil on the cards.
       c. Only one student wrote a 3 on a card.

8. Which two numbers is there an equally likely chance of picking?
   _____ and _____

GRAPHS, DATA, AND PROBABILITY

WEEK
DAY
1
THIRTY

Name _____

Help Lizzie figure out the outcomes of flipping a coin.

Lizzie flipped a coin 10 times. She recorded the results in a tally chart.

Side of Coin	Times Flipped
Heads	⁄⁄⁄⁄ |
Tails	||||

1. How many times did Lizzie flip heads? _____

2. How many times did Lizzie flip tails? _____

3. Use the data to fill in the table.

Side of Coin	Times Flipped
Heads	
	4

4. Based on Lizzie's flips, which outcome is more likely? _____

GRAPHS, DATA, AND PROBABILITY

WEEK
DAY
2
THIRTY

Name _____

Help Mark record the outcomes of spinning a spinner.

Mark spun this spinner 50 times. He landed on black 10 times. He landed on a gray section 7 times. He landed on white 20 times. He landed on a striped section 13 times.

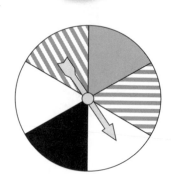

Fill in the table using Mark's data.

Color	Times Spinner Landed
Black	
	7

GRAPHS, DATA, AND PROBABILITY

WEEK
DAY
3
THIRTY

Name _____

Fill in the blanks with words from the box. Use each word once.

| tally marks   possible outcomes   records   tally chart |

1. Jasmine flips a coin 100 times. She _____ the results of each flip by writing it down.

2. Jasmine writes the result of each flip. She uses a set of lines called _____.

3. Sometimes Jasmine's coin lands on heads. Sometimes it lands on tails. Those are the two _____.

4. Jasmine records her data in a _____.

GRAPHS, DATA, AND PROBABILITY

WEEK
DAY
4
THIRTY

Name _____

Fill in the blanks with words from the box. Use each word once.

Lands on	1	2	3	4	5	6
Number of times	IIII	HHt	IIII		III	IIII

| outcome   possible   tally mark   tally chart |

1. There are 6 _____ outcomes on a number cube.

2. Miguel recorded each _____ of his experiment.

3. Miguel put all of his data in a _____.

4. Miguel drew one _____ next to each number when he rolled that number.

GRAPHS, DATA, AND PROBABILITY

Name _____

Ian put 4 marbles in a box. Each marble was a different color: red, blue, green, or yellow. Ian shook the box. Then he closed his eyes and took out one marble. He wrote the color of the marble. Then he put the marble back in the box. He did this 25 times. Ian recorded the outcomes on a notepad.

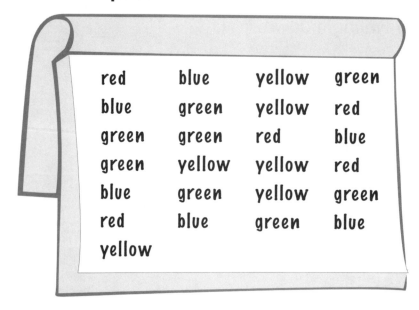

red	blue	yellow	green
blue	green	yellow	red
green	green	red	blue
green	yellow	yellow	red
blue	green	yellow	green
red	blue	green	blue
yellow			

I. How many times did Ian pick a red marble? _____ times

2. How many times did Ian pick a green marble? _____ times

3. How many times did Ian pick a yellow marble? _____ times

4. How many times did Ian pick a blue marble? _____ times

5. Use the space below to show Ian's outcomes in a tally chart.

GRAPHS, DATA, AND PROBABILITY

Name _____

Use the pictograph to complete each sentence.

Students Who Have Pets in Mr. McCarthy's Class

Pets	Students Who Have the Type of Pet
Dog	☺ ☺ ☺ ☺ ☺
Cat	☺ ☺ ☺ ☺ ☺ ☺ ☺
Hamster	☺ ☺ ☺
Bird	☺ ☺ ☺ ☺
Lizard	☺

Key ☺ = 1 student

1. _____ students have a hamster.

2. The pet that most students have is a _____.

3. _____ students have a bird.

4. The pet that the fewest students have is a _____.

GRAPHS, DATA, AND PROBABILITY

Name _____

Use the bar graph to complete each sentence.

Gold Medals in the 2004 Olympics

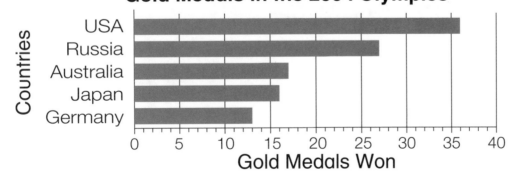

1. _____ won the most gold medals.

2. _____ won 13 gold medals.

3. Russia won _____ gold medals.

4. Australia won _____ more gold medal(s) than Japan.

GRAPHS, DATA, AND PROBABILITY

Name _____

Circle the word that describes the phrase.

1. information that you collect
   a. answers   **b.** data   **c.** graphs

2. a way to organize data
   a. a table   **b.** an outcome   **c.** a key

3. a graph that uses bars to show data
   a. a tally chart   **b.** a pictograph   **c.** a bar graph

4. a graph that uses pictures or symbols to show data
   a. a tally chart   **b.** a pictograph   **c.** a bar graph

5. the part of a pictograph that tells you what each picture means
   a. title   **b.** key   **c.** column

GRAPHS, DATA, AND PROBABILITY

Name _____

Answer the questions about the parts of the pictograph.

Money Raised in a Bake Sale

Grade	Money Raised
First	💰 💰 💰 💰
Second	💰 💰 💰
Third	💰 💰 💰 💰
Fourth	💰 💰 💰

Key 💰 = $2

1. The title of the graph is _____.
2. The key shows that each 💰 means _____.
3. The picture 💰 means _____.
4. You can tell that the _____ grade raised the most money.

GRAPHS, DATA, AND PROBABILITY

Name _____

Marcia surveyed the students in the third grade. She asked each student to name his or her favorite color. She recorded the data in the table below. Then she used the data to make the bar graph. She does not know how to finish her table. This is what she has so far.

Red	Blue	Green	Yellow	Purple	Orange
20			10		10

1. Five students said that purple was their favorite color. Fill in the data in Marcia's table.

2. Fifteen students said that blue was their favorite color. Fill in the data in Marcia's table.

3. Ten students said that green was their favorite color. Fill in the data in Marcia's table.

Marcia started making a bar graph with her data. Here is what she has so far.

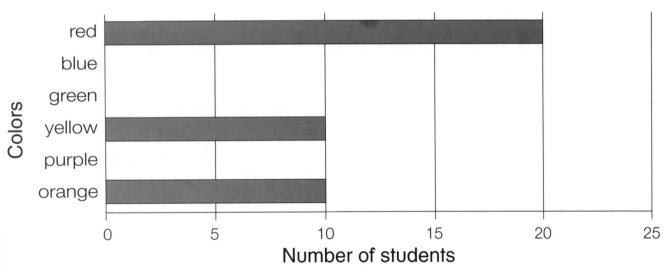

Favorite Colors

4. Fill in the bar graph for the number of students who said blue, green, and purple.

GRAPHS, DATA, AND PROBABILITY

Name _____

Read Jason's experiment. Then, use the results to circle each answer.

Jason puts 5 red marbles, 3 blue marbles, and 2 yellow marbles in a bag. He reaches in and takes out a marble. He records the color in a notebook. Then he puts the marble back. He repeats his experiment 10 times.

1. About how many times will Jason pick a red marble?
   a. 2   **b.** 5   **c.** 10

2. About how many times will Jason pick a yellow marble?
   a. 2   **b.** 5   **c.** 10

3. About how many times will Jason pick a marble that is *not* blue?
   a. 0   **b.** 3   **c.** 7

4. Jason repeats his experiment 20 times. About how many times will he pick a blue marble?
   a. 3   **b.** 6   **c.** 23

GRAPHS, DATA, AND PROBABILITY

Name _____

Complete each sentence. Use the results of Keisha's experiment.

Keisha spins a spinner 100 times. She lands on a red space 77 times. She lands on a blue space 20 times. She lands on a pink space 3 times.

1. Keisha spins the spinner one more time. She will likely land on

   a _____ space.

2. Keisha spins the spinner one more time. It is _____ that she land on a green space.

3. Keisha spins the spinner 10 more times. She should land on a blue space about _____ times.

GRAPHS, DATA, AND PROBABILITY

WEEK
DAY
3
THIRTY TWO

Name _____

Fill in the blanks with words from the box. Use each word once.

| probability | predict | outcome | likely | impossible |

1. The _____ tells the chance of an event happening.

2. The result of a probability experiment is called an _____.

3. We use probability to show us how _____ an outcome is.

4. Probability experiments can help us _____ if an event will happen.

5. If there is no chance an event will occur, it is _____.

GRAPHS, DATA, AND PROBABILITY

WEEK
DAY
4
THIRTY TWO

Name _____

Circle the word that completes each sentence.

1. The chance that an event will happen is its _____.
   a. probability   **b.** outcome   **c.** decision

2. If you roll a six-sided number cube there are six possible _____.
   a. probabilities   **b.** outcomes   **c.** decisions

3. The chance of an event happening is $\frac{8}{10}$. It is _____ to happen.
   a. likely   **b.** unlikely   **c.** certain

4. The chance of an event happening is $\frac{2}{8}$. It is _____ to happen.
   a. likely   **b.** unlikely   **c.** certain

GRAPHS, DATA, AND PROBABILITY

Name _____

Use the results from Jessica's experiment. Then, answer the questions.

Jessica used this spinner to do a probability experiment. She spun it 100 times. Each time she wrote down the outcome. Some of the data is recorded in the table.

Number	1	2	3	4
Times spun	42	29		

1. How many different outcomes are possible when Jessica spins the spinner? _____

2. How many times did Jessica spin the spinner in total? _____

3. How many times did Jessica land on the number 1? _____

4. Jessica wants to predict what her next spin will be. What fraction shows the probability of her landing on the number 1? (Hint: Use your answers from questions 2 and 3.) _____

5. How many sections are on the spinner? _____

6. How many sections on the spinner have the number 4? _____

7. What fraction shows the probability of Jessica landing on the number 4? (Hint: Use your answers from questions 5 and 6.) _____

8. Predict about how many times the spinner landed on 4. _____

9. Predict about how many times the spinner landed on 3. _____

GRAPHS, DATA, AND PROBABILITY

Name _____

A. Use the data in the table to complete the bar graph.

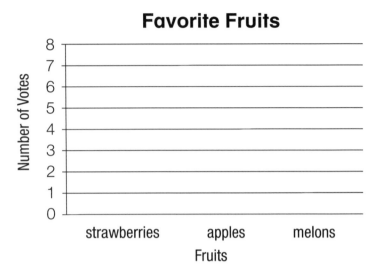

Favorite Fruits

Favorite Fruits	
strawberries	8
apples	5
melons	5

B. Fill in the blanks with numbers from the box.

0	1	9

1. The chance an unlikely event will happen is _____ out of 10.

2. The chance an likely event will happen is _____ out of 10.

3. The chance an impossible event will happen is _____ out of 10.

C. Find each word about probability. Look up, down, diagonally, backward, and forward. Circle each word.

data	event	certain	unlikely	table	outcome	predict

O	A	N	B	C	A	U	W	P	Q
U	T	C	I	D	E	R	P	K	U
T	D	A	T	A	B	L	E	Z	B
C	J	Y	V	Z	T	N	E	V	E
O	D	R	O	C	E	R	X	Q	U
M	H	U	N	L	I	K	E	L	Y
E	T	J	A	K	S	L	F	C	G

PATTERNS

Name _____

Look at the pattern. Circle the shape that comes next.

1. △ ☐ △ ☐ △ ☐ △ ☐

    a. ☐   **b.** ◯   **c.** △

2. ☐ ▢ ☐ ▢ ☐ ▢ ☐ ▢

    a. ☐   **b.** ▢   **c.** △

3. ⬠ ▭ △ ⬠ ▭ △ ⬠ ▭ △

    a. ▭   **b.** ⬠   **c.** △

PATTERNS

Name _____

Look at the pattern. Draw the shape that comes next.

1. ◿ ◺ ◿ ◺ _____

2. △ △ ▭ △ △ ▭ _____

3. ◿ ◯ ◯ ◿ ◯ ◯ ◿ _____

PATTERNS

Name _____

Fill in the blanks with words from the box. Use each word once.

predict	rule	pattern	sun	star

Ron looked at the tiles in his bathroom. They looked like this.

Ron saw that the group of shapes repeated. That means it had a

_____. Its _____ was star, _____, moon. A tile was

missing. Ron wanted to _____ what came next. The next shape

in the pattern is a _____.

PATTERNS

Name _____

Fill in the blanks with words from the box. Use each word once.

pattern	extend	repeat	predict	shape

☐ ◯ ☐ ◯ ☐ ◯

1. These shapes form a pattern because they _____.

2. If you know the rule of a pattern, you can _____ the next shape.

3. The next _____ in the pattern should be a square.

4. When numbers or shapes repeat, they form a _____.

5. If you add on the next shape, you _____ the pattern.

PATTERNS

Name _____

Mr. Garden drew patterns on the board. First he used dots. Then he used shapes. Use the pattern to answer each question.

1. Which shows the rule of Mr. Garden's pattern?
   Circle the correct answer.

   a. ●●   ●●   **b.** ●●   ●●●   **c.** ●●●   ●●●

2. Extend the pattern. Draw the next set of dots. _____

3. Write the pattern as a number pattern.

4. Write the next number in the number pattern. _____

Here is Mr. Garden's shape pattern.

5. Which is the rule for this pattern? Circle the correct answer.

   a. 3 triangles, 2 circles

   b. 2 circles, 2 triangles

   c. 2 triangles, 3 circles

6. Draw the next set of shapes in the pattern.

_____

PATTERNS

Name _____

Circle the rule for the number pattern.

1. 2, 4, 6, 8   **a.** Multiply by 2.   **b.** Subtract 2.   **c.** Add 2.

2. 1, 2, 3, 4   **a.** Add 1.   **b.** Multiply by 2.   **c.** Divide by 2.

3. 15, 13, 11, 9   **a.** Add 1.   **b.** Add 2.   **c.** Subtract 2.

4. 6, 12, 18, 24   **a.** Add 6.   **b.** Multiply by 2.   **c.** Add 4.

5. 5, 10, 15   **a.** Add 10.   **b.** Add 1.   **c.** Add 5.

PATTERNS

Name _____

Continue each pattern. Fill in the blank.

1. 100, 90, 80, _____

2. 40, 41, 42, _____

3. 18, 21, 24, _____

4. 56, 55, 54, _____

5. 35, 40, 45, _____

PATTERNS

Name _____

Fill in the blanks with words from the box. Use each word once.

subtract	next	add	rule

1. The first numbers in a number pattern are 4, 5, 6.

The _____ number is 7.

2. The first numbers in a number pattern are 3, 6, 9. The rule of this

pattern is _____ 3.

3. The first numbers in a pattern are 11, 10, 9. The rule of this

pattern is _____ 1.

4. The numbers 18, 20, 22, 24 make a pattern. The _____ is to go

up by 2.

PATTERNS

Name _____

Fill in the word that tells about each pattern. Use a word from the box. Use each word once.

ones	twos	threes	fives	tens

1. 8, 10, 12, 14   This pattern shows counting by _____.

2. 5, 10, 15, 20   This pattern shows counting by _____.

3. 40, 50, 60, 70   This pattern shows counting by _____.

4. 2, 3, 4, 5   This pattern shows counting by _____.

5. 11, 14, 17, 20   This pattern shows counting by _____.

PATTERNS

Name _____

Every morning on the way to school, Matthew walks by a potter's studio. The potter makes vases from clay. On Monday, there are 5 vases in the potter's window. On Tuesday, there are 8 vases. On Wednesday, there are 11 vases. On Thursday, there are 14 vases.

If the potter keeps up at the same rate and doesn't sell any vases, how many will there be when Matthew goes to school on Friday?

Answer the questions. Use the pattern of vases that Matthew sees.

1. Write the number of vases Matthew sees each day.

   Monday: _____   Tuesday: _____

   Wednesday: _____   Thursday: _____

2. Are the numbers in this pattern going up or going down? Circle the correct answer.

   going up   going down

3. What is the difference between each number in the pattern? _____

4. Do you have to add or subtract to get the next number in the pattern? Circle the correct answer.

   add   subtract

5. The potter keeps making vases at the same rate. The number pattern continues. How many vases will Matthew see on Friday? _____

PATTERNS

Name _____

Match the related number sentences.

1. $27 \div 3 = 9$

2. $8 \times 5 = 40$

3. $63 \div 9 = 7$

4. $2 \times 6 = 12$

5. $42 \div 7 = 6$

a. $7 \times 6 = 42$

b. $7 \times 9 = 63$

c. $12 \div 6 = 2$

d. $9 \times 3 = 27$

e. $40 \div 8 = 5$

PATTERNS

Name _____

Which number sentence is in the same fact family? Circle it.

1. $7 \times 5 = 35$

    a. $36 \div 6 = 6$ **b.** $35 \div 7 = 5$ **c.** $7 \times 6 = 42$

2. $20 \div 2 = 10$

    a. $10 \times 2 = 20$ **b.** $10 \times 20 = 200$ **c.** $20 \div 4 = 5$

3. $12 \div 4 = 3$

    a. $12 \div 3 = 4$ **b.** $12 \times 3 = 36$ **c.** $12 \times 4 = 48$

4. $6 \times 3 = 18$

    a. $6 \times 18 = 108$ **b.** $18 \div 3 = 6$ **c.** $6 \div 3 = 2$

PATTERNS

Name _____

Fill in the blanks with words from the box. Use each word once.

fact family	dividend	quotient	related	product

1. In a division number sentence, you divide the _____ by the divisor.

2. The answer in a division problem is the _____.

3. 4 × 5 = 20 and 20 ÷ 5 = 4 are _____ number sentences.

4. The answer in a multiplication problem is the _____.

5. Related multiplication and division form a _____.

PATTERNS

Name _____

Circle the word that completes each sentence.

1. In the number sentence 32 ÷ 4 = 8, the _____ is 8.

    a. quotient   **b.** dividend   **c.** divisor

2. In the number sentence 32 ÷ 8 = 4, the _____ is 8.

    a. quotient   **b.** dividend   **c.** divisor

3. In a division sentence, the divisor multiplied by the quotient equals the _____.

    a. quotient   **b.** dividend   **c.** divisor

4. In the number sentence 8 × 4 = 32, the _____ is 32.

    a. product   **b.** dividend   **c.** factor

PATTERNS

Name _____

Use fact families to show ways to group Ernie's trucks.

1. Ernie has 15 toy trucks. He wants to separate them into 3 equal groups. Draw 3 circles around the trucks to show how he can make 3 equal groups.

2. Write a number sentence that shows this division.

_____

3. Ernie wants to separate his trucks into 5 equal groups. Draw 5 circles around the trucks to show how he can make 5 equal groups.

4. Write a number sentence that shows this division.

_____

5. What related multiplication number sentences can you write using the numbers 3, 5, and 15?

_____

_____

PATTERNS

Name _____

Count the number in each picture.

1.

   Number of legs: _____   _____   _____

2.

   Number of fingers: _____   _____   _____

3.

   Number of wheels: _____   _____   _____

© Weekly Reader Corporation

PATTERNS

Name _____

Circle each correct answer.

1. How many legs would 4 horses have?

   a. 4   **b.** 12   **c.** 16

2. How many fingers would 4 hands have?

   a. 16   **b.** 20   **c.** 25

3. How many wheels would 4 tricycles have?

   a. 10   **b.** 12   **c.** 14

© Weekly Reader Corporation

PATTERNS

Name _____

Circle the correct answer.

1. A box of raisins has 40 raisins. Which expression does *not* show how many raisins are in 5 boxes?

   a. 5×40 **b.** $40 + 5$ **c.** $40 + 40 + 40 + 40 + 40$

2. Cows have 4 stomachs. How can you find how many stomachs 6 cows have?

   a. Add 4 and 6.   **b.** Multiply 4 and 6.   **c.** Divide 6 by 4.

3. A cat has 20 claws. Which expression does *not* show how many claws 4 cats have?

   a. 4×20 **b.** $20 + 20 + 20 + 20$ **c.** $20 + 4$

PATTERNS

Name _____

Complete each sentence. Circle the correct answer.

1. Numbers in a pattern increase by 5.
   The number that comes _____ 25 is 30.   before   after

2. Numbers in a pattern increase by 7.
   The number that comes _____ 28 is 21.   before   after

3. Numbers in a pattern increase by 4.
   The number that comes before 71 is _____.   67   75

4. Numbers in a pattern decrease by 11.
   The number that comes after 41 is _____.   30   52

PATTERNS

Name _____

A spaceship weighs 50 tons. It goes around the Earth every 2 hours. It goes around the Earth 2 times every 4 hours. It goes around the Earth 3 times every 6 hours. The pilot wants to find the pattern for his ship.

1. The ship goes around the Earth 4 times in _____ hours.

2. The ship goes around the Earth 5 times in _____ hours.

3. Write the number of hours it takes for the ship to make trips around the Earth.

    1 trip around Earth: _____ hours

    2 trips around Earth: _____ hours

    3 trips around Earth: _____ hours

    4 trips around Earth: _____ hours

    5 trips around Earth: _____ hours

4. How can you find out how long it takes the ship to go around the Earth 10 times?

    _____

5. The ship has to complete a mission. It needs to go around the Earth 120 times. How many hours will it take?

    _____

PATTERNS

Name _____

A. Look at each pattern. Draw the next shape.

1. ○ ◿ ○ ◿ _____

2. ⇦ ⇧ ⇨ ⇦ ⇧ ⇨ _____

B. Look at the number sentences. Then, follow the directions.

$$14 \div 2 = 7 \qquad 2 \times 7 = 14$$

1. Circle the quotient.

2. Draw a square around the product.

3. Underline the factors.

4. Draw a dot over the divisor.

5. Draw a rectangle around the dividend.

C. Write the next number in each pattern. Then, write the matching letter in the box. The letters spell out the answer to this riddle.

Riddle: *What kind of cat always breaks the rules?*

6 = E	12 = C	16 = H	20 = H	30 = T	32 = E	62 = A

1. 3, 6, 9, _____ ☐

2. 13, 14, 15, _____ ☐

3. 14, 20, 26, _____ ☐

4. 9, 8, 7, _____ ☐

5. 21, 24, 27, _____ ☐

6. 41, 48, 55, _____ ☐

7. 5, 10, 15, _____ ☐

Answer: ____ ____ ____ ____ ____ ____ ____
  1   2   3   4   5   6   7

ANSWER KEY

Month 1: Place Value

Week 1
Day One: 1. 147; 2. 2,007; 3. 3,169; 4. 8,311; 5. 4,642
Day Two: 1. 5,357; 2. 9,979; 3. 1,131; 4. 1,640; 5. 6,004
Day Three: 1. nine thousand, five hundred twenty-nine; 2. seven thousand, five hundred three; 3. six thousand, ten; 4. one thousand, five hundred seventeen; 5. three thousand, one hundred forty-two
Day Four: 1. hundreds; 2. word form; 3. place value; 4. thousands; 5. standard form
Day Five: 1. 1,250 feet; 2. one thousand, four hundred fifty-one feet; 3. one thousand, three hundred eighty-one feet; 4. one thousand, six hundred sixty-seven feet; 5. The first 1 is in the thousands place, and the second is in the ones place. The values are one thousand and one.

Week 2
Day One: 1. 8,000; 2. 8; 3. 80; 4. 800; 5. 80
Day Two: 1. 800; 2. 40; 3. 1,000; 4. 6; 5. 500
Day Three: 1. hundreds place; 2. ones place; 3. thousands place; 4. tens place; 5. ones place.
Day Four: 1. 1; 2. 3; 3. 3; 4. 5; 5. 0
Day Five: 1. Earth; 2. Mercury; 3. 9; 4. 900; 5. 4,000 and 4

Week 3
Day One: 1. >; 2. <; 3. >; 4. <; 5. <
Day Two: 1. 576; 2,899; 3,001; 9,241; 2. 903; 4,769; 4,772; 8,005; 3. 78; 952; 1,355; 8,067; 4. 9; 99; 2,363; 9,999
Day Three: 1. less than; 2. greater than; 3. equal to; 4. less than; 5. less than
Day Four: 1. >; 2. =; 3. >; 4. =; 5. <
Day Five: 1. No, because the digits in the thousands place are both 1; 2. No, because the digits in the hundreds place are both 7; 3. Yes, because the digit in the tens place is 2 for John's school and 3 for Rafael's school; 4. No, you don't need to compare the digits in the ones place because the digits in the tens place are different; 5. 1,728 < 1,736

Week 4
Day One: 1. 6,527; 2. 1,902; 3. 3,776; 4. 9,218; 5. 5,001
Day Two: 1. 7,000 + 100 + 90 + 9; 2. 9,000 + 300 + 10 + 3; 3. 1,000 + 100 + 20 + 7; 4. 4,000 + 900 + 50 + 2; 5. 6,000 + 200 + 80 + 4
Day Three: 1. standard form, 7,000 + 500 + 40 + 7; 2. word form, 2,026; 3. expanded form, 3,761
Day Four: 1. hundreds; 2. hundreds, tens; 3. thousands; 4. tens; 5. ones
Day Five: 1. 7,000; 400; 50; 6; 2. 1,000; 200; 50; 3; 3. 2,000; 800; 9; 4. 3,000; 100; 80

Month 1 Review
A. 1. <; 2. >; 3. =
B. 1. less, hundreds; 2. less, thousands; 3. greater, ones
C. Order is: Nile 4,180 mi, Amazon 3,912 mi, Mississippi-Missouri 3,710 mi, Yangtze 3,602 mi, Ob 3,459 mi, Yellow 2,900 mi

Month 2: Addition & Subtraction

Week 5
Day One: 1. 979; 2. 1,787; 3. 8,998; 4. $9,877; 5. 8,889
Day Two: 1. 2,568; 2. 5,689; 3. 9,879
Day Three: 1. addition; 2. sum; 3. addends; 4. sum
Day Four: 1. sum, $7,679; 2. plus, 5,754; 3. altogether, 2,898; 4. total number, 4,898
Day Five: 1. b; 2. 4,322 and 3,626; 3. 4,322 + 3,626 = __; 4. addends;

5. 4,322
+ 3,626
‾‾‾‾‾
7,948

6. 1,341
+ 1,341
‾‾‾‾‾
2,682

Week 6
Day One: 1. 321; 2. $5,524; 3. 3,622; 4. 1,115; 5. $4,113
Day Two: 1. 2,112; 2. $2,211; 3. 1,122; 4. 3,512
Day Three: 1. How much is left; 2. $3,043; 3. How many more; 4. 2,221
Day Four: 1. subtract; 2. 1,113; 3. difference; 4. 5,560 from 8,675
Day Five: 1. "What is the difference;" 2. Detroit; 3. 2,284; 4. 2,018; 5. 2,018 from 2,284;
6. 2,284
− 2,018
‾‾‾‾‾
266

7. 266 miles

Week 7
Day One: 1. 6,862; 2. $9,358; 3. 9,210; 4. 8,217; 5. $9,820
Day Two: 1. 6,393; 2. 7,711; 3. $9,115; 4. 8,023; 5. $8,285
Day Three: 1. altogether; 2. add; 3. sum; 4. addends; 5. regroup
Day Four: 1. altogether, 3,313; 2. How many … in both years, 9,315; 3. total number, 8,261; 4. the sum of both accounts, $3,631
Day Five:

1. 3,902
+ 2,879

2. 2 + 9 = 11; You must regroup 11 ones as 1 ten 1 one; 3. 1 + 7 = 8. You do not need to regroup. You can write 8 in the sum in the tens place; 4. 9 + 8 = 17. You must regroup 17 hundreds as 1 thousand 7 hundreds. 5. 1 + 3 + 2 = 6. You write a 6 in the thousands place in the sum; 6. 6,781

Week 8
Day One: 1. 1,632; 2. $5,043; 3. 82; 4. 1,687; 5. $2,123
Day Two: 1. 2,737; 2. 1,891; 3. $4,883; 4. $412; 5. 1,029
Day Three: 1. are left; 2. more; 3. difference
Day Four: 1. take away; 2. minus; 3. subtract; 4. difference; 5. how many more
Day Five: 1. subtraction;

2. 1902
– 1886

3. You must regroup to make 12 in the ones place. To do that, you must regroup from the hundreds place, leaving 800 in the hundreds place and 90 in the tens place; 4. Answers will vary. Possible answer: When you regroup, you name numbers in a different way. For example, you might regroup numbers from the tens place as numbers in the ones place; 5. 16 years

Month 2 Review
A. 1. $5,949; 2. 7,899; 3. $5,878; 4. 9,475; 5. $1,528
B. 1. 1,331 from 3,669; 2,338; 2. 1,574 from 3,669; 2,095
C.

	¹4				
²6	1	3	³5		
	3		5		
⁴1	0	1	⁵2		
		⁶7	7	9	9
			8		
			8		

Month 3: Multiplication

Week 9
Day One: 1. 15; 2. 0; 3. 42; 4. 9; 5. 36; 6. 40
Day Two: Review students' tables.
Day Three: 1. b; 2. a; 3. c; 4. a; 5. b
Day Four: 1. multiplication; 2. factors; 3. sum; 4. product
Day Five: 1. 4; 2. 5; 3. multiply; 4. 4 and 5; 5. 20; 6. 20

Week 10
Day One: 1. 102; 2. 639; 3. 95; 4. 162; 5. 432
Day Two: 1. 168; 2. 46; 3. 256
Day Three: 1. a; 2. c; 3. a; 4. c
Day Four: 1. c; 2. c; 3. b; 4. a
Day Five: 1. $5; 2. 52; 3. b.

4.
  52
x 5

5. $260
6.
  52
x 6
312

Week 11
Day One: 1. 2,463; 2. 0; 3. 1,430; 4. 3,787; 5. 2,298
Day Two: 1. 1,716; 2. 1,449; 3. 4,750; 4. 2,296
Day Three: 1. c; 2. b; 3. a; 4. a
Day Four: 1. b; 2. c; 3. c.
Day Five: 1. 2,000; 2. 4; 3. 570; 4. multiplication; 5. 4 and 570; 6. 4, 570, 2,280; 7. 2,280; 8. yes.

Week 12
Day One: 1. 10,224 ; 2. 17,310; 3. 60,488; 4. 36,508; 5. 12,627
Day Two: 1. 15,358; 2. 50,166; 3. $12,160; 4. $17,098
Day Three: 1. a; 2. c; 3. a; 4. a; 5. a
Day Four: 1. multiply; 2. product; 3. factors; 4. factors
Day Five: 1. b; 2. c; 3. 4,848; 4. 8; 5. 4,848 and 8; 6. 38,784

Month 3 Review
A. 1. 12; 2. 285; 3. 3,020; 4. 6,672; 5. 14,518
B. 1. multiply; 2. product; 3. factor
C. 1. 750; 2. 1,350; 3. Box B

Month 4: Division

Week 13
Day One: 1. 9; 2. 8; 3. 6; 4. 9; 5. 7
Day Two: 1. 3; 2. 8; 3. 3 miles
Day Three: 1. dividend; 2. divisor; 3. quotient; 4. dividend; 5. divisor; 6. quotient
Day Four: 1. 2, 12, 6; 2. 7, 42, 6; 3. 1, 16, 16; 4. 8, 40, 5; 5. 7, 14, 2
Day Five: 1. 54; 2. 42; 3. 6; 4. b; 5. divide; 54, 6; 6. divide; 42, 6; 7. 9; 8. 7; 9. 9 − 7 = 2

Week 14
Day One: 1. 58; 2. 23; 3. 67; 4. 728; 5. 66
Day Two: 1. 34; 2. 82; 3. 68; 4. 86
Day Three: 1. 200; 2. 360; 3. 10
Day Four: 1. 2, 196, 98; 2. 7, 609, 87; 3. 4, 220, 55; 4. 6, 144, 24; 5. 3, 195, 65
Day Five: 1. 380, 4; 2. 455, 5; 3. b; 4. divide 380 by the number 4; 5. divide 455 by the number 5; 6. 95; 7. 91; 8. a

Week 15
Day One: 1. $4; 2. $5; 3. $37; 4. $2
Day Two: 1. $48; 2. $53; 3. $43; 4. $68
Day Three: 1. $20; 2. $50; 3. $30; 4 $80
Day Four: 1. glove; 2. price; 3. total; 4. each
Day Five: 1. $96; 2. division; 3. 96 ÷ 3 = $32; 4. $108; 5. division; 6. 108 ÷ 4 = $27; 7. blue paint

Week 16
Day One: 1. 4; 2. 7; 3. 9; 4. 1
Day Two: 1. 5,913; 2. 862; 3. 46; 4. 51
Day Three: 1. 41; 2. 60; 3. 181; 4. 0; 5. factor, 266
Day Four: 1. 30; 2. 308; 3. 9; 4. divisor, 1; 5. dividend, 900
Day Five: 1. $8; 2. $240; 3. $8 × box = $240; 4. c; 5. a; 6. 30

Month 4 Review
A. 1. 9; 2. 91; 3. 149
B. 1. 9; 2. 8; 3. 24
C.

U	M	B	R	E	L	L	A	S
1	2	3	4	5	6	7	8	9

Month 5: Geometry

Week 17
Day One: 1. pentagon; 2. quadrilateral; 3. hexagon; 4. triangle; 5. rectangle
Day Two: 1. octagon; 2. hexagon; 3. square; 4. pentagon; 5. quadrilateral
Day Three: 1. c; 2. b; 3. b; 4. c; 5. a
Day Four: 1. 4, 4; 2. 8, 8; 3. 6, 6; 4. 5, 5; 5. 3, 3
Day Five: 1. L shape made of two rectangles; 2. 6; 3. 6; 4. Check students' drawings; 5. 4; 6. 4

Week 18
Day One: 1. e; 2. d; 3. b; 4. a; 5. c
Day Two: 1. no; 2. no; 3. yes; 4. no; 5. yes
Day Three: 1. similar; 2. congruent; 3. square; 4. size; 5. shape
Day Four: 1. congruent; 2. similar; 3. Check students' drawings.
Day Five: 1. c; 2. c; 3. b; 4. No, because all squares have four equal sides and four right angles. Therefore, all squares are similar.

Week 19
Day One: 1. yes; 2. yes; 3. no; 4. yes; 5. no
Day Two:
1–4. Check students' drawings.
Day Three:
1–5. Check students' drawings.
Day Four: 1. true; 2. false; 3. true; 4. false
Day Five:
1–5. Check students' drawings.

Week 20
Day One: 1. c; 2. e; 3. b; 4. a; 5. d;
Day Two: 1. 6; 2. 8; 3. 2, 4. 5, 5; 5. 1
Day Three: 1. face; 2. vertex; 3. edge; 4. vertices; 5. prism
Day Four: 1. cylinder; 2. pyramid; 3. cube; 4. cone; 5. rectangular solid
Day Five: 1. b; 2. c; 3. b; 4. a; 5. a

Month 5 Review
A. 1. hexagon; 2. quadrilateral; 3. pentagon; 4. cube
B.
1–3. Check students' drawings.
C. Check students' drawings.

Month 6: Measurement

Week 21
Day One: 1. 11 centimeters; 2. 6 centimeters; 3. 9 centimeters; 4. 3 centimeters; 5. 7 centimeters
Day Two: 1. 5 inches; 2. 3 inches; 3. 4 inches; 4. 2 inches; 5. 4 inches
Day Three: 1. longer; 2. feet; 3. length; 4. centimeters; 5. inches
Day Four: 1. d; 2. e; 3. a; 4. c; 5. b
Day Five: bookmark: 4 inches; key: 5 inches; paper clip: 2 inches; pen: 7 inches; race car: 3 inches; thumbtack: 1 inch
From shortest to longest: thumbtack, paper clip, race car, bookmark, key, pen

Week 22
Day One: 1. 20 feet; 2. 18 inches; 3. 14 feet; 4. 14 yards
Day Two: 1. 18 cm; 2. 26 m; 3. 40 cm; 4. 24 m
Day Three: 1. perimeter; 2. length; 3. sides; 4. multiply; 5. add
Day Four: 1. 160 meters; 2. 160 feet; 3. 120 inches; 4. 130 yards
Day Five: 1. 4 inches; 2. 6 inches; 3. 4 inches; 4. 6 inches; 5. b.; 6. 4 + 6 + 4 + 6; 7. 20 inches; 8. 20 inches

Week 23
Day One: 1. 8; 2. 9; 3. 12; 4. 12; 5. 15
Day Two: 1. 8; 2. 18; 3. 24; 4. 27
Day Three: 1. volume; 2. perimeter; 3. area; 4. solid; 5. polygon
Day Four: 1. area; 2. volume; 3. volume; 4. area
Day Five: 1. 9; 2. 4; 3. b; 4. a; 5. 36; 6. b.; 7. 26

Week 24
Day One: 1. b; 2. b; 3. a; 4. b
Day Two: 1. capacity; 2. length; 3. length; 4. weight; 5. capacity
Day Three: scale; pounds; gallon; cup; weight
Day Four: 1. a; 2. c; 3. a; 4. c; 5. c
Day Five: 1. miles, kilometers; 2. gallons, liters; 3. pounds, kilograms; 4. cups, liters

Month 6 Review
A. 1. 24 meters; 2. 52 yards; 3. 8 feet
B. 1. a; 2. c; 3. b
C.

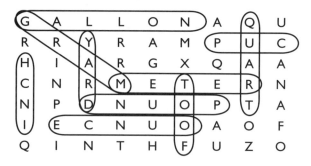

Month 7: Fractions

Week 25
Day One: 1. c; 2. e; 3. d; 4. a; 5. b
Day Two:
1–4. Check students' figures.
Day Three: 1. fraction; 2. denominator; 3. numerator; 4. equivalent
Day Four: 1. b; 2. b; 3. b; 4. a
Day Five: 1. 5 of 10 pencils colored; 2. 5/10; 3. 4 out of 10 pencils colored; 4. 4/10; 5. No, because 5/10 does not equal 4/10; 6. Henry; 7. 5; 8. 5/10 = 5/10

Week 26
Day One: 1. 4/8; 2. 3/4; 3. 4/6; 4. 4/5; 5. 4/10
Day Two: 1. 7/8; 2. 4/6; 3. 5/8; 4. 4/5; 5. 8/10
Day Three: 1. b; 2. a; 3. c; 4. a
Day Four: 1. add; 2. plus; 3. like; 4. denominator; 5. numerator
Day Five: 1. 1/3; 2. 1/3; 3. a; 4. 2/3 gallon; 5. 10; 6. 2; 7. 2/10; 8. 1; 9. 1/10; 10. 2/10 + 1/10 = 3/10

Week 27
Day One: 1. c; 2. a; 3. b; 4. c; 5. c
Day Two: 1. 3/8; 2. 6/10; 3. 1/4; 4. 1/5; 5. 2/6
Day Three: 1. a; 2. c; 3. b; 4. a
Day Four: 1. denominator; 2. equivalent; 3. minus; 4. difference
Day Five: 1. 6; 2. 3; 3. 3/6; 4. 2; 5. 2/6; 6. 3/6 − 2/6 = 1/6; 7. 3/6 should be shaded; 8. 1/6

Week 28
Day One: 1. <; 2. >; 3. <; 4. <; 5. >; 6. >
Day Two:
1. 4/6
2. 1/3
3. 2/3
4. 2/5
5. 7/8

Day Three: 1. c; 2. a; 3. c; 4. a; 5. b
Day Four: 1. greater; 2. equals; 3. less; 4. less; 5. greater
Day Five: 1. >; 2. <; 3. <; 4. =; 5. >

Month 7 Review
A. 1. 4/8; 2. 5/10; 3. 5/6
B. add; denominator; like fractions; numerator
C. 1. 5/8 = I; 2. 5/10 = T; 3. 7/8 = S; 4. 2/4 = B, 5. 3/5 = A, 6. 1/3 = N, 7. 5/6 = K, 8. 7/10 = S; Answer to riddle: ITS BANKS

Month 8: Data, Probability, and Graphs

Week 29
Day One: 1. unlikely; 2. certain; 3. likely
Day Two: 1. c; 2. c; 3. c
Day Three: 1. b; 2. b; 3. c; 4. a; 5. a
Day Four: 1. likely; 2. unlikely; 3. certain; 4. unlikely
Day Five: 1. 15; 2. 10; 3. b; 4. 15; 5. 0; 6. a; 7. b; 8. 1 and 2

Week 30
Day One: 1. 6; 2. 4;
3. Check students' tables.
4. heads
Day Two: Check students' tables.
Day Three: 1. records; 2. tally marks;
3. possible outcomes; 4. tally chart
Day Four: 1. possible; 2. outcome; 3. tally chart;
4. tally mark
Day Five: 1. 5; 2. 8; 3. 6; 4. 6
6.

red	blue	green	yellow
‖‖‖	‖‖‖ I	‖‖‖ III	‖‖‖ I

Week 31
Day One: 1. 3; 2. cat; 3. 4; 4. lizard
Day Two: 1. The USA; 2. Germany; 3. 27; 4. 1
Day Three: 1. b; 2. a; 3. c; 4. b; 5. b
Day Four: 1. Money Raised in a Bake Sale; 2. 2 dollars;
3. 1 dollar; 4. First
Day Five: 1–3. Check students' tables.
4. Check students' graphs.

Week 32
Day One: 1. b; 2. a; 3. c; 4. b
Day Two: 1. red; 2. impossible; 3. 2
Day Three: 1. probability; 2. outcome; 3. likely; 4. predict;
5. impossible
Day Four: 1. a; 2. b; 3. a; 4. b
Day Five: 1. 4; 2. 100; 3. 42; 4. 42/100; 5. 10; 6. 1; 7. 1/10; 8. 10; 9. 20

Month 8 Review
A. Check students' graphs.
B. 1. 1; 2. 9; 3. 0
C.

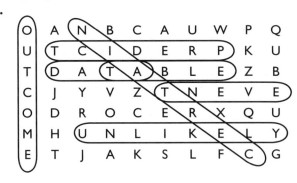

Month 9: Patterns

Week 33
Day One: 1. c; 2. a; 3. b
Day Two: Check students' drawings.
Day Three: pattern, rule, sun, predict, star
Day Four: 1. repeat; 2. predict; 3. shape; 4. pattern;
5. extend
Day Five: 1. b; 2. Check students' work.; 3. 2, 3, 2, 3, 2;
4. 3; 5. a; 6. Check students' work.

Week 34
Day One: 1. c; 2. a; 3. c; 4. a; 5. c
Day Two: 1. 70; 2. 43; 3. 27; 4. 53; 5. 50
Day Three: 1. next; 2. add; 3. subtract; 4. rule
Day Four: 1. twos; 2. fives; 3. tens; 4. ones; 5. threes
Day Five: 1. Monday: 5, Tuesday: 8, Wednesday: 11,
Thursday: 14; 2. going up; 3. 3; 4. add; 5. 17

Week 35
Day One: 1. d; 2. e; 3. b; 4. c; 5. a
Day Two: 1. b; 2. a; 3. a; 4. b
Day Three: 1. dividend; 2. quotient; 3. related; 4. product;
5. fact family
Day Four: 1. a; 2. c; 3. b; 4. a
Day Five: 1. 3 circles, 5 trucks in each; 2. $15 \div 3 = 5$ or
$15 \div 5 = 3$; 3. 5 circles, 3 trucks in each; 4. $15 \div 3 = 5$
or $15 \div 5 = 3$; 5. $3 \times 5 = 15$ or $5 \times 3 = 15$

Week 36
Day One: 1. 4, 8, 12; 2. 5, 10, 15; 3. 3, 6, 9
Day Two: 1. c; 2. b; 3. b
Day Three: 1. b; 2. b; 3. c
Day Four: 1. after; 2. before; 3. 67; 4. 30
Day Five: 1. 8 hours; 2. 10 hours; 3. 2, 4, 6, 8, 10;
4. Multiply the number of trips around the Earth by
2 hours for each trip: $10 \times 2 = 20$ hours;
5. $120 \times 2 = 240$ hours

Month 9 Review
A. 1–2. Check students' drawings.
B. 1. a circle around 7 in division problem
2. a square around the 14 in multiplication problem
3. underline the 2 and the 7 in multiplication problem
4. a dot over the 2 in division problem
5. a rectangle around the 14 in division problem
C. 1. 12, C; 2. 16, H; 3. 32, E; 4. 6, E; 5. 30, T. 6. 62, A; 7. 20, H
Answer to riddle: CHEETAH